Discrimination
by Design

LESLIE KANES WEISMAN

Discrimination by Design

A Feminist Critique of the Man-Made Environment

UNIVERSITY OF ILLINOIS PRESS
Urbana and Chicago

Library of Congress Cataloging-in-Publication Data

Weisman, Leslie.
    Discrimination by design : a feminist critique of the man-made
environment / Leslie Kanes Weisman.
        p.   cm.
    Includes bibliographical references and index.
    ISBN 0-252-01849-4 (cl)
    1. Architecture and women—United States.   I. Title.
NA2543.W65W45   1992
720'.1'03—dc20   91-16024
                                                          CIP

This book is dedicated to all those who dare to imagine a world at peace, in which differences are truly celebrated and all living things matter.

Contents

Acknowledgments

I am grateful to many people for their support while I was working on this book; to my friend and colleague Dale Spender for her consistently clear-headed advice, sense of humor, and the model of her own impressive scholarship; to Carole S. Appel, my editor at the University of Illinois Press, for her candor, thoughtfulness, professionalism, and skillful tutelage in the technical aspects of publishing; and to Carol Bolton Betts, who copyedited my manuscript with care and sensitivity. I also owe my heartfelt thanks to Sharon Good for nurturing me through the impossible times with patience, generosity, and understanding; and to Connie Murray for her unfailing encouragement. They have made the experience of sisterhood a daily part of my life.

Thanks are also due to the New Jersey Institute of Technology for granting me sabbatical leave to work full time on the research for this book; to Alice Fahs for her extensive and valuable editorial comments on the early drafts; to Nina Prantis and my students Jamie Malanga and Maggie Denlea for their assistance with the illustrations; to Filiz Ozel for deciphering and translating various computerized drafts of the manuscript; and to Renada Woodford for typing the text. Susana Torre enthusiastically supported both my original book proposal and the completed manuscript, and offered important criticism in between. Gerda R. Wekerle provided a thoughtful critique of the organizational and conceptual framework; Jan Bishop contributed helpful advice on the section about environments designed for childbirth; and Ellen Perry Berkeley was always available for professional guidance and personal support when I needed it most.

I am also indebted in immeasurable ways to the women with whom I cofounded the Women's School of Planning and Architecture in 1974: Katrin Adam, Ellen Perry Berkeley, Noel Phyllis Birkby, Bobbie Sue Hood, Marie Kennedy, and Joan Forrester Sprague, and the countless other WSPA sisters, especially Harriet Cohen, who joined us over the years. It was within this creative environment that we first raised the question of the relevance of architecture and planning to feminism and began to formulate some answers.

Finally my loving thanks go to my mother, Mollie Kanes, my sister, Susan Kanes, and my father, the late Marvin Kanes, who have supported my choice to live the kind of life that made writing this book possible.

But ultimately this book owes its existence to the energy and consciousness of the women's movement. It is from that source of inspiration and scholarship that its contents and the sensibility within its pages are derived.

Introduction
The Spatial Dimensions of Feminism

On New Year's Eve of 1971, at a time when radical activism was at the epicenter of the growing women's movement, seventy-five women took over an abandoned building owned by the city of New York. They issued the following statement on 29 January:

> Because we want to develop our culture,
> Because we want to overcome stereotypes,
> Because we refuse to have "equal rights"
> in a corrupt society,
> Because we want to survive, grow, be ourselves,
>
> We took over a building to put into action with women
> those things essential to women—health care,
> child care, food conspiracy, clothing and book
> exchange, "gimme women's shelter," a lesbian
> rights center, inter-arts center, feminist
> school, drug rehabilitation.
>
> We know the City does not provide for us.
> Now we know the City will not allow us to
> provide for ourselves.
> For this reason we were busted.
> We were busted because we are women acting
> independently of men, independently of the system . . .
> In other words, we are women being revolutionary.
>
> (Fifth Street Women, *The Militant*)

The Fifth Street Women clearly understood that the appropriation of space is a political act, that access to space is fundamentally related to social status and power, and that changing the allocation of space is inherently related to changing society. Despite this early awareness, today among feminists there is little understanding of the spatial dimensions of "women's issues" and how a knowledge of these dimensions can help us map the mental and physical terrain of our struggle for human justice and social transformation. An awareness of how relations among human beings are shaped by built space can help all of us to comprehend more fully the experiences of our daily lives and the cultural assumptions in which they are immersed.

It is easy to accept unthinkingly the man-made landscape as a neutral background. It is not so easy to understand the environment as an active shaper of human identity and life's events. In this regard there is a striking parallel between space and language. We are taught to imagine that the language we use is value-free and neutral; that "man" and "he" are generic terms meant to include "women." Feminist linguists have developed convincing arguments to the contrary, revealing how male-centered language perpetuates women's invisibility and inequality.[1]

Space, like language, is socially constructed; and like the syntax of language, the spatial arrangements of our buildings and communities reflect and reinforce the nature of gender, race, and class relations in society. The uses of both language and space contribute to the power of some groups over others and the maintenance of human inequality.

Architecture thus defined is a record of deeds done by those who have had the power to build. It is shaped by social, political, and economic forces and values embodied in the forms themselves, the processes through which they are built, and the manner in which they are used. Creating buildings involves moral choices that are subject to moral judgment.

It is within this social context of built space that I believe feminist criticism and activism have a profoundly important role to play. Toward those ends, I hope this book will contribute to furthering our understanding of why the acts of building and controlling space have been a male prerogative; how our physical surroundings reflect and create reality; and how we can begin to challenge and change the forms and values encoded in the man-made (by which I mean, throughout this book, the *male-made*) environment, thereby fostering the transformation of the sexist and racist conditions that define our lives.

What are the spatial dimensions of pornography, reproductive freedom, and the Equal Rights Amendment? The feminist with a spatial consciousness instinctively knows that the uterus is the primordial human space and that the invasion of a woman's body privacy by anti-abortion legislators, advocates of forced sterilization, rapists, and greedy pornographers is the most violent form of trespassing. He or she understands that a woman's sexuality is defined by her spatial location; that the "virtuous" woman is found in the nuclear family house, the "whore" in the house of ill-repute and in the embodiment of any woman who dares to walk the streets at night.

Such a feminist sees that the obstetrical ward is designed to isolate women from the human community as though childbirth were a contagious disease. The person who approaches the question of equal rights for women with a spatial consciousness realizes that women will never be equal in the public workplace until the private domestic workplace is redesigned to reflect the awareness that we are all, irrespective of gender, responsible for the places in which we live.

Yet a feminist analysis of the man-made environment as a form of social oppression, an expression of social power, a dimension of history, and a part of women's struggle for equality has come much later than comparable critiques of, for example, employment, health care, and family life. The reason for this tardiness is understandable. Such an evaluation would logically be initiated by women architects and planners and there are simply fewer of them than there are women in other fields.

In the United States in 1970 only 3.7 percent of some 57,081 registered architects were women. By 1980 the number had risen to 8.3 percent.[2] In the United Kingdom in 1978, 5.2 percent of architects were women.[3] There are generally more women in urban planning, perhaps because it is a newer field, but the numbers are nothing to brag about. For example, among the 25,000 planners at work in America in 1980, about 15 percent were women.[4] While the percentages slowly increased throughout the 1980s, women remain dramatically underrepresented in both disciplines. Further, there is no way to determine the numbers within this small constituency who are committed to feminism and are directing their work accordingly.[5]

To the limited extent that professional architects and planners, be they women or men, have anything to say about what gets built, where, how, and for whom, men do most of the talking. Women are typically clustered in the lower-paying, lower-status jobs. These decisions are more frequently made by investment builders, engineers, developers, governmental agencies, city managers, the real estate industry, corporations, and financial institutions. Few women are in important decision-making positions in these occupations and businesses either.

Since the early 1980s, significant contributions to the study of women and environments have been added to those of architects and planners by feminist academicians in anthropology, cultural and urban geography, technology, environmental psychology, urban sociology, and urban and architectural history. Yet research to date represents only the smallest beginnings of scholarship, consisting primarily of fact finding, problem definition, descriptive case studies, and anecdotal narratives. There are few longitudinal or comparative studies, and the integration of new data within the existing framework of feminist or urban theory has yet to be accomplished.[6]

However, I find these circumstances far from discouraging. They are simply inherent in any work that is both innovative and cross-disciplinary. The emergence of more fully developed theories and models on women and environments is inevitable if those doing the research continue to bring the perceptions and experiences of their womanhood and, for both women and men, their feminism, to the ways in which they see the world and understand it.

How does built space contribute to human oppression? Can it contribute to human liberation? If we could build anew our cities, neighborhoods, workplaces, and dwellings in ways that fostered relationships of equality and environmental wholeness, what would they be like? And how can we imagine such a radically different landscape while we live in a society that is not yet liberated? In this book I raise and explore these questions by explaining how buildings and communities are designed and used to reinforce the social place held by different members of society.

In the first chapter, "The Spatial Caste System: Design for Social Inequality," I introduce the concepts of dichotomy and territoriality as theoretical spatial devices used to construct and defend the patriarchal symbolic universe. Both concepts reappear as underpinnings in all the other chapters. In chapter 2, "Public Architecture and Social Status," I show how gender and economic class, and the social power and status associated with them, are translated into the spatial organization, use, and visual appearance of large-scale public buildings: skyscrapers, department stores, shopping malls, and maternity hospitals (which I contrast with birth centers, and private homes relative to the type of birth experience each environment promotes).

I explain in chapter 3, "The Private Use of Public Space," how public space—from the city's "Porno Strip" and "Skid Row" to the neighborhood park and the nation state—is claimed, controlled, and experienced differently according to one's social position. I also explain how and why feminists are using public space as an arena of protest against violence and militarism.

In chapter 4, "The Home as Metaphor for Society," I analyze how the social caste system, designed to separate women and men, black and white, servant and served, is encoded in the floorplans, image, and use of domestic architecture, from private houses to public housing. I discuss wife battering within the spatial context of the family home, describe the problems and possibilities of designing shelters for victims of domestic violence, and propose a feminist housing agenda.

In chapter 5, "Redesigning the Domestic Landscape," I explain how the spatial and social dichotomization of the private house and public workplace, and the inexorable enforcement of the primacy of the male-headed family, have together created a dramatic misfit between conventional housing and neighborhoods and today's diverse households characterized by changing conditions of work and family life. I describe how existing housing could be adapted and new housing designed to support individuals and families at different stages in the human life-cycle, from childhood to widowhood.

I speculate in the final chapter, "At Home in the Future," about the nature of dwellings, neighborhoods, cities, and workplaces in two contrasting scenarios of the future, one based on the development of human potential and relationships of equality, the other on the development of technology and the perpetuation of social inequality. I review how feminist writers and activists from the 1970s described nonsexist utopian communities, comment on the difficulties inherent in imagining the physical forms they might assume, and compare them to drawings made by women illustrating their environmental fantasies. I conclude the book by explaining the role I think women should play in designing a society that honors human difference, and in shaping an architecture that will house those values.

Organizing the text has involved years of intuitive searching for patterns among seemingly disparate fields of study; of plotting points of intersection on the patriarchal map of social injustice beneath which lie opportunities for in-depth research and discovery. The results are admittedly idiosyncratic and subjective. My point of view is unequivocally feminist. I am indebted to many scholars named in the text for the insights and information I found in their published and unpublished works; but I assume singular responsibility for my interpretations.

Readers who are conversant with feminist literature will encounter many recognizable places within these pages. What well-read feminists will find enlightening, I hope, is a reinterpretation of familiar themes from a spatial perspective. Readers who are architects, planners, geographers, and environmental and social scientists will, I believe, find that this book furthers their awareness of the inescapable connections between their work and the quality of women's lives, and motivates them to use their expertise to benefit women and other socially disadvantaged groups.

NOTES

1. Dale Spender, in her book *Man Made Language* (London: Routledge and Kegan Paul, 1980), offers the following explanation: "If man does represent the species then the symbol should be applicable to the activities of all human beings. . . . Can we say without a clash of images that man devotes more than forty hours a week to housework or that man lives an isolated life when engaged in childrearing in our society? A note of discord is struck by these statements because man—despite the assurances of male grammarians—most definitely means male and evokes male imagery" (156).

2. The American Institute of Architects, *1983 AIA Membership Survey: The Status of Women in the Profession*, Draft, 13 April 1984 (Washington, D.C.: The American Institute of Architects).

3. Michael P. Fogarty, Isobel Allen, and Patricia Walters, *Women in Top Jobs, 1968–1979* (London: Heinemann Educational Books, 1981), 223, as quoted in Matrix Collective, *Making Space: Women and the Man-Made Environment* (London: Pluto Press, 1984), 37.

4. Jacqueline Leavitt, "Women as Public Housekeepers," Papers in Planning PIP18 (New York: Columbia University Graduate School of Architecture and Planning, 1980), 42–43.

5. For information on feminist activism and criticism within architecture and planning and the history of architectural education and practice and women's current place within it, the following readings are recommended. In the United States: Ellen Perry Berkeley, "Women in Architecture," *Architectural Forum* 137 (September 1972): 45–53; idem, "Architecture: Towards a Feminist Critique," in *New Space for Women*, ed. Gerda R. Wekerle, Rebecca Peterson, and David Morley (Boulder, Colo.: Westview Press, 1980), 205–18; Doris Cole, *From Tipi to Skyscraper* (Boston: I Press), 1973; Susana Torre, "Women in Architecture and the New Feminism," in *Women in American Architecture: An Historic and Contemporary Perspective*, ed. Susana Torre (New York: Whitney Library of Design, 1977), 148–51; Leslie Kanes Weisman and Noel Phyllis Birkby, "The Women's School of Planning and Architecture," in *Learning Our Way: Essays in Feminist Education*, ed. Charlotte Bunch and Barbara Pollack (Trumansburg, N.Y.: Crossing Press, 1983), 224–45; Leslie Kanes Weisman, "A Feminist Experiment: Learning from WSPA, Then and Now," in *Architecture: A Place for Women*, ed. Ellen Perry Berkeley with Matilda McQuaid (Washington, D.C.: Smithsonian Institution Press, 1989), 125–33. (Berkeley's collection of original essays is recommended in its entirety.) Forthcoming is Leslie Kanes Weisman, "Designing Differences: Women and Architecture," in *The Knowledge Explosion: Generations of Feminist Scholarship*, ed. Dale Spender and Cheris Kramarae (Oxford: Pergamon Press, Athene Series). In the United Kingdom: Susan Francis, "Women's Design Collective,"

Heresies, "Making Room: Women and Architecture," issue 11, vol. 3, no. 3 (1981):17; Matrix Collective, *Making Space: Women and the Man-Made Environment* (London: Pluto Press, 1984). In Australia, write to the following organizations: The Association of Women in Architecture, c/o Dimity Reed, 27 Malin St., Qew, Victoria 3101; Constructive Women, P.O. Box 473, New South Wales 2088. In Canada, *Women and Environments*, an excellent international newsletter, is published quarterly by the Centre for Urban and Community Studies, 455 Spadina Ave., Toronto, Ontario M5S2G8. Write to the center for subscription rates.

6. Two excellent review essays that document women and environments research are available: Dolores Hayden and Gwendolyn Wright, "Architecture and Urban Planning," *Signs: A Journal of Women in Culture and Society* (Spring 1976): 923–33; and Gerda R. Wekerle, "Women in the Urban Environment," *Signs: A Journal of Women in Culture and Society*, special issue, "Women and the American City," supplement, vol. 5, no. 3, (Spring 1980): 188–214. In addition, Gerda R. Wekerle, Rebecca Peterson, and David Morley describe the emergence of women and environments as a field of study in the introduction to their anthology *New Space for Women*, 1–34. Two other anthologies are also available: an interdisciplinary collection, *Building for Women*, ed. Suzanne Keller (Lexington, Mass.: Lexington Books, 1981), and a collection of studies in cultural anthropology, *Women and Space: Ground Rules and Social Maps*, ed. Shirley Ardener (New York: St. Martin's Press, 1981). For an examination of the scholarship on feminist geography, see *Her Space, Her Place: A Geography of Women*, ed. Mary Ellen Mazey and David R. Lee (Washington D.C.: Association of American Geographers, 1983); and *Geography and Gender: An Introduction to Feminist Geography*, ed. Women and Geography Study Group of the IBG (London: Hutchinson, 1984).

1

The Spatial Caste System: Design for Social Inequality

Building the Symbolic Universe:
The Dichotomization of Space

Our buildings, neighborhoods, and cities are cultural artifacts shaped by human intention and intervention, symbolically declaring to society the place held by each of its members. The wealthy live in penthouse apartments; the poor live in housing projects. Each group knows on which side of the tracks it belongs.

Physical space and social space reflect and rebound upon each other. Both the world "out there" and the world inside ourselves depend upon and conform to our socially learned perceptions and values. Neither is understandable without the other. We keep a "professional distance" from our employees, students, patients, and clients. We "look up" to another person as a symbol of respect and "look down" on someone to signify disrespect or disdain.

Space provides an essential framework for thinking about the world and the people in it. We are constantly made aware of this function of space by the numerous spatial terms we use in our ordinary conversation.[1] Expressions such as "high society," "narrow-mindedness," "climbing the ladder of success," "political circles," "everything has its place," and so on, remind us that social life is "shaped," events "take place," and people exist in relationship to space and time.[2]

We simply do not understand who we are until we know where we are. This understanding is not the same for everyone. In societies where gender roles, race, and class are strongly differentiated, women and men, black and white, rich and poor will adopt different values and attitudes toward the environment and will experience and perceive the environment in different ways.

The cognitive map or mental picture of the physical environment that each of us carries around in our head is largely dependent upon the social space we occupy. This is true among all societies and in all settings. For example, when Inuits on Southampton Island were asked to draw maps of their surroundings, the men, who are hunters, recorded the island's outline with its harbors and inlets; the women's maps were made of points that indicated the location of settlements and trading posts. Both, however, were equally accurate.[3]

In urban societies, the gender-based division of labor ensures that the housebound suburban homemaker will not have the same image of the environment as her wage-earning husband who spends his day in a steel-and-glass office building in the central city. Similarly, patterns of race and class segregation guarantee that the children of New York City's Harlem will not connect the "uptown" Park Avenue they know with the "downtown" Park Avenue of opulent apartment buildings and clean, tree-lined sidewalks.

There is, then, an ongoing dialectical relationship between social space and physical space. Both are manufactured by society, as is metaphysical space—our moral and religious beliefs. Collectively, these three spatial realms constitute the symbolic universe that structures human experience and defines human reality. Far from being absolute, the symbolic universe varies greatly among different cultures since it is subjectively created. Yet by its very nature the symbolic universe seems to be an inevitable totality that makes our everyday roles, values, and behaviors legitimate.[4]

Logically, those who have the power to define their society's symbolic universe have the power to create a world in which they and their priorities, beliefs, and operating procedures are not only dominant, but accepted and endorsed without question by the vast majority. In patriarchal societies where men are by definition the dominant group, social, physical, and metaphysical space are the products of male experience, male consciousness, and male control. Further, man-made space encodes and perpetuates white male power and superiority and the inferiority and subordination of women and minorities, from confinement to the master bedroom and the back of the bus to exclusion from the corporate boardroom.

In understanding the structuring of the patriarchal symbolic universe, the concept of the dichotomy is essential. Classifying people into opposing groups of rich/poor, white/black, young/old, straight/gay, and male/female creates a social system that justifies and supports human exploitation and white male supremacy. For in each case, one group is afforded power and status and the other rendered powerless and inferior. Dichotomies, in addition to defining social space, define the way we conceptualize metaphysical space (heaven and hell) and physical space (for example, workplace and dwelling).

What follows in this chapter is an exploration first of how spatial dichotomies operate at three different scales: the human body, built space, and patterns of human settlement (cities and suburbs); and second, how the concept of territoriality—the claiming and defending of social, built, and metaphysical space—is used to protect and reinforce these dichotomies.

Bodyscape as Landscape

Different cultures throughout time have used the cardinal points of the human body—top and bottom, right and left, and front and back—as an analogic model to structure social, built, and cosmological space. The spatial relations among these points structure both our physical world and our social world view. We grovel at the feet of the powerful; equals look each other in the eye; and the person who "heads" an organization is the highest authority. In addition to social status, we associate moral qualities with somatic space. A person assumes full stature when "upright"; a person who "backs down" is a feckless coward.

Distance, direction, and location are all defined in relation to the human bodyscape. Something close by is within a "stone's throw" or within "shouting distance." There are twelve inches in a "foot"; a yard is a "stride"; a mile is one thousand paces. Time is also defined anthropocentrically. The future lies "ahead" of us; the past lies "behind" us.

The use of spatial terms derived from the body is absorbed into the structure of language, thought, and reality to help language "place" abstract concepts like time and distance in a system of relations that make them more accessible to human understanding.[5] Similarly, in virtually every society the categorization of ambient body space into complementary and unequally valued coordinates is used to symbolize and reinforce the basic social distinctions between male and female. The superior coordinates—top, right, and front—are associated with male; the inferior coordinates—bottom, left, and back—with female. The work of countless ethnographers indicates that this dual classification is universal, and that inequalities between the sexes, though most likely described as differences, are symbolized in the organization and use of space at all scales, from the house, to village and city, to heaven above where God the Father reigns supreme.

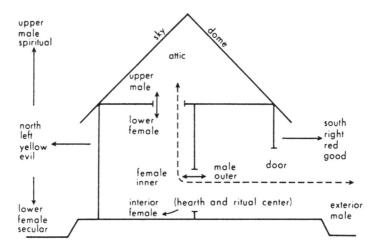

Figure 1. Cosmic and social order in the Atoni house of Indonesian Timor, symbolically depicting the dual classification of the body coordinates into male/positive, female/negative categories. Clark E. Cunningham, "Order in the Atoni House," in *Right and Left: Essays in Dual Symbolic Classification*, ed. Rodney Needham (Chicago: University of Chicago Press, 1973), 217, fig. 7. Reproduced courtesy the University of Chicago Press.

Cross-cultural examples of the spatial relations of male/superiority and female/inferiority abound. In Indonesian society (see fig. 1) space is organized into two categories: (1) left, female, seaside, below, earth, spiritual, downward, behind, west; (2) right, male, mountainside, above, heaven, worldly, upward, in front, east.[6] Men are associated with life which emanates from the mountain and upperworld, while women are associated with death, sickness, and calamity which emanates from the underworld of the sea. In Chinese cosmology, Yang, the male principle, is associated with fire, and is directed upward, joyful, and phallic; Yin, the female principle, is associated with water, passivity, and fear. To the Chinese, water symbolizes the feminine unconscious. Immersion in water extinguishes fire and the masculine consciousness. It means death.[7]

In Western society, geographic space associated with women is also characterized by a deadening torpor while male space is characteristically vivifying. The dichotomization of American cities and suburbs provides a recognizable example. We tend to associate urban life with cultural and intellectual activities, power, aggression, danger, meaningful work, important world events, and with men. Feminine suburbia is comparatively safe, domestic, tranquil, close to nature, and mindless. "The suburbs, in this sense, conform to the Freudian conception of femininity: passive, intellectually void, instinctually distracted," writes Barry Schwartz, author of *The Changing Face of the Suburbs* (1976).[8]

The use of body space as a cultural blueprint for designing sexual inequality is also manifest in a strong social bias toward the right side. The anthropologist Robert Hertz wrote in his now famous essay *The Pre-Eminence of the Right Hand* (1909): "Society and the whole universe has a side which is sacred, noble, and precious and another which is profane and common: a male side, strong and active, and another, female, weak and passive; or in two words, a right side and a left side."[9]

The right side of the body, controlled by the left hemisphere of the brain, functions in a linear, logical, assertive, rational manner. It creates the concept of causality and remembers how to speak and use words. The right hemisphere of the brain controls the left side of the body, which functions in a holistic, intuitive, receptive, and affective manner. It perceives whole patterns and remembers the lyrics of songs. Because society values the former set of attributes and devalues the latter, the right side is called "masculine," the left side "feminine."[10]

Obviously, both women and men are born with bi-hemispheric brains. Yet society expects the members of each sex to develop only half their human potential, and those halves are not equally valued. No wonder so many children who were born left-handed, until recently, were browbeaten by parents and teachers into writing right-handed. In a society where maleness is the norm, left-handedness is an embarrassing deviance. It is not coincidental that those considered to be "correct" are called "right."

Not surprisingly, in social space the guest of honor sits at the right side of the host; and in cosmological space Christ sits at the right hand of the Father. Further, Jesus is depicted in the Last Judgment with his right hand raised toward the brightness of Heaven and his left hand pointing downward to the darkness of Hell.[11]

There are some notable exceptions to this preference for right-sidedness. Among the ancient Egyptians, Mongols, and Chinese, the left side is sacred and the right side profane. However, within these societies, the left side is considered male, the right side, female.

For example, the Chinese reverse the left side to the masculine, and the right side to feminine, because their social and cosmological space, depicted in the layout of ancient imperial cities, places the ruler and his royal palace in the center of the plan facing south and the sun. As a result, the ruler's left side is east, where the sun rises (light), and his right side west, where the sun sets (darkness). With logical consistency, the Chinese consider the front of the body to be luminous/male and the back of the body to be dark/female.[12] Not accidentally, women in traditional China walked behind, in the shadows of their male superiors.

The distinction between the front of the body as a symbol of dignity and the back of the body as a symbol of ignobility is widespread. Many people everywhere turn their backs on those they wish to disregard, and they believe that courageous people face their problems; up-front people are honest and trustworthy, and backward people are acceptable subjects for jokes and ridicule. Objective physical space also takes on these somatic values. Adults and guests enter homes through the front door while delivery people, servants, and children enter through the back.

An equally abundant number of examples can be found in which height is a symbol of superior status, masculinity, and power. Important executive offices are located on the top floors of corporate towers from which their occupants can overlook the cities their enterprises dominate and control. The rich and powerful buy prime real estate that commands the most visual space—from penthouse apartments to hilltop sites—assured of their social position every time they look out their windows and see the world at their feet.

Throughout history, important buildings, such as temples, have been placed on platforms, and important people, for example, kings and popes, have been seated in elevated chairs called thrones. Height is such an important symbol of dominance and power that in Washington, D.C., skyscrapers over ninety feet tall are forbidden by law so that the nation's capitol building reigns as the highest structure.[13] If ancient obelisks and columns were built to celebrate the military conquests of departed warriors, twentieth-century skyscrapers were built to celebrate the economic conquests of the "captains of commerce," with unabashed competition among the corporate giants to build the tallest building as a symbol of ultimate superiority.

But the idea that height symbolizes masculine superiority originates in patriarchal cosmological space, not architectural space. Many cultures dichotomize and value differently the worship of a heaven and a "sky father" and the earth and an "earth mother." Wherever the father reigns, he does so from above, and height becomes a sacred male symbol. When the earth goddess is revered, the soil and valley are sacred. For example, the Cretan palaces of the goddess-worshipping Mycenaeans of ancient Greece were designed to adapt to the forces of the earth. The ideal building site was an enclosed valley which acted as a natural megaron or "sheltering womb." The conquering Dorians, however, who supplanted the Mycenaean earth mother with their male, thunder-wielding sky god Zeus, dominated the landscape with monumental temples and strongholds built on the tops of the highest mountains. Mount Olympus itself was considered Zeus's northern embodiment.[14]

To the patriarchs, the mountain was sacred; it brought earthly man closer to his heavenly father. The Old Testament of the Hebrews recounts how Moses received the Ten Commandments from God on top of Mount Sinai. Ancient towers, pillars, spires, obelisks, and ziggurats—like the legendary 200-foot Tower of Babel—were built by men as sacred acts, intended to connect the earth to heaven.[15] The higher the elevation, the more sacred the space. Rabbinical literature teaches that Israel stands higher above sea level than any other land. Islamic tradition teaches that the Kaaba, the most sacred sanctuary, is located at both the center and the "navel" of the world as well as the highest point.[16] In colonial America, the pious Governor of the New World, John Winthrop, commanded his pilgrim flock to build the New Jerusalem as described in the Book of Revelations, "as a City on a Hill."[17]

Thus have cardinal points been used to design a world that places man "on top" and "out front" and woman "on the bottom" and "way behind," thereby communicating and perpetuating messages of inequality between the sexes.

The Sexual Symbolism of Architectural Form

Another spatial dichotomy related to the human body is the use of architectural form to symbolize biologically different sexual anatomies and socially different gender roles for women and men. Freudian psychology made us aware of the unconscious human tendency to fashion phallic and womblike artifacts. Among certain cultures the fabrication of penis objects and fecund female forms is both conscious and literal. Indeed, whether consciously produced or not, such symbols are widespread.

However, the interpretation of virtually all vertical structures as phallic symbols and all rounded or enclosed constructions as breasts or wombs is an unjustifiable obsession with symbolism where none exists. Even Freud admitted "sometimes a cigar is just a cigar."[18] Further, to assume that designing flamboyant, aggressively tall buildings is an inherently male act and designing modestly scaled, sensually curved buildings an inherently female act is to delimit and stereotype both woman and man to our mutual detriment.

It is the totality of one's self that forms the world in the process of comprehending it. The inference of metaphorical meaning from built form depends upon one's cultural and psychological associations. It is a product of gender, race, class, and biological experience, among other experiences. Thus, it is easy to understand why an observer of a building or work of art may infer a different meaning than that intended by the designer.

Are sexual analogies and metaphors inherent in architecture? Or are they inherent in the language we use to write and talk about architecture? Some theoreticians interpret architecture as representational space, a language that expresses meanings outside itself such as social and economic structure or "masculine/feminine" values or qualities. Others view architecture as a language that refers only to itself and its own history, communicating a purely formal vocabulary, grammar, and syntax. Whether meaning is inside or outside of architecture, the projection of meaning is inherent in both the creation of built form and the act of observing it.

Since time immemorial the plan of the body and the plan of society have together been responsible for the shaping of buildings and human settlements. For example, the historian Lewis Mumford explains that in the matriarchal hoe culture of the early Neolithic village, the nurturing "arts of life" that had made woman supreme—menstruation, copulation, and childbirth—were imprinted in the spatial form of the village itself: "In the house and in the oven, the byre and the bin, the cistern, the storage pit, the granary . . . the wall and the moat, and all inner spaces from the atrium to the cloister, house and village, eventually the town itself were woman writ large."[19] Mumford contrasts this with the later patriarchal plow culture that gave rise to the city-state in which male processes—"aggression and force," "the ability to kill," and a "contempt for death"—prevailed. He describes the mark these changes in human society left on the whole landscape: "Male symbolism and abstractions show themselves in the insistent straight line, the rectangle, the firmly bounded geometric plan, the phallic tower and the obelisk. . . . while the early cities seem largely circular in form, the ruler's citadel and the sacred precinct are more usually enclosed by a rectangle."[20]

No single architectural form better incarnates the union of social roles and sexual anatomy than the American skyscraper, the pinnacle of patriarchal symbology and the masculine mystique of the big, the erect, and the forceful. Allusions to male sexuality are unavoidable when referring to the skyscraper which, according to the lexicon of the architect, consists of a "base," "shaft," and "tip."

While vertical structures have, throughout history, served as sacred "masculine" icons, the house has been inextricably associated with women, especially women's bodies. References to the house as a "birthplace," a "cozy nest," a "sheltering womb," and a "vessel for the soul" are widespread in most cultures. Caves, the earliest dwellings, were "nature's womb."

Oliver Marc, author of *The Psychology of the House* (1977), has hypothesized that man "left the cave out of a deep evolutionary imperative." The first houses "he" built were recreations of the womb which paralleled the birth process while symbolizing a separation from it. The square house that followed marked the next evolutionary step, the birth of individuality. Women, apparently incapable of transcending their biology, continued to build womb houses, according to Marc.[21] Freudian theory supports this pejorative view of women by equating a "return to the womb" with an incomplete psychosexual development.[22]

Literature is full of images of the house as a "maternal womb." In his autobiography, the psychoanalyst Carl Jung describes the house he built for himself on Lake Zurich, a primitive round tower of stone: "The feeling of repose and renewal that I had in this tower was intense from the start. It represented for me the maternal hearth."[23] Henri Basco describes a house during a storm: "The house clung to me like a she-wolf, and at times, I could smell her odor penetrating maternally to my very heart. That night she was really my mother."[24] Writers and poets, women and men alike, romanticize the house filled with children's laughter and describe with sorrow and pity the "empty nest," which, like a woman's menopausal body, is seen to be tragically barren.

Women's social and biological roles, and the human attributes and emotions associated with them, merge in the strong and cherished image of the dwelling. In many modern works of art by women, images of the house, woman's body, and the role of house/wife merge symbiotically in a vivid social commentary on the house as woman's prison. Artist Louise Bourgeois depicted themes of containment, anxiety, and the frustrated desire to escape in a series of paintings and drawings done in the 1940s entitled *Femme/Maison* (fig. 2). In a project entitled *Womanhouse* (1971) feminist artists Judy Chicago and Miriam Schapiro, with their students at the California Institute of the Arts, portrayed the house as a repository of female experience, oppression, and fantasy. The women created a collection of satirical

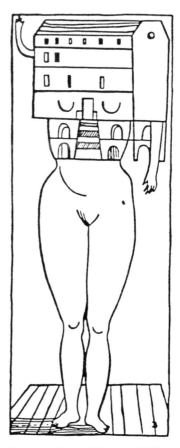

Figure 2. *Femme/Maison*, 1947,
Louise Bourgeois. Reproduced
courtesy Louise Bourgeois.

domestic environments within a rundown house they renovated
themselves that included a bridal staircase, a menstruation bathroom,
a dollhouse room, a linen closet "prison" from which a nude woman-
nequin was struggling to emerge, an elaborate bedroom in which a
seated woman perpetually brushed her hair and applied makeup, and
a "nurturant," fleshy pink kitchen in which plastic fried eggs on the
ceiling turned into breasts as they moved down the walls, taking on
the feeling of skin and becoming mother/nurturer/kitchen simultaneously (fig. 3).

"A house is not a home" without mother and the warm family relationships she engenders. The personal, "feminine" enclosure of the

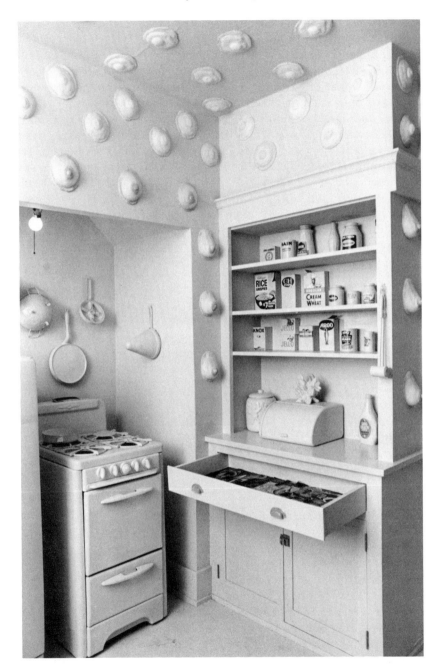

Figure 3. "Nurturant Kitchen," Vicki Hodgetts, Robin Weltsch, and Susan Frazier. From *The Womanhouse Project*, 1971. Photograph courtesy Miriam Schapiro.

private house stands in metaphorical contrast to the anonymous, "masculine" upward thrust of our public towers.

In associating the workplace with male power, impersonalization, and rationality, and the home with female passivity, nurturance, and emotionalism, distinctly different behaviors in public and private settings, and in women and men, have been fostered. The result is the creation of a symbolic universe that holds women privately responsible for the care, repair, and renewal of human life in a world they do not essentially control, and assigns to men the public responsibility for running the houses of government where they have become more concerned with the nuclear race than the human race. Under these conditions, we can no longer afford to confine the "female attributes" to the home and family; for men, insofar as they embody this patriarchal dichotomy, have created a world that is dangerous for everyone, including themselves. Healing this schism through new spatial arrangements that encourage the integration of work and play, intellect and feeling, action and compassion, is a survival imperative.

The City of Man versus Mother Nature

At an even larger scale the dichotomization of cities, metaphorically associated with "man" and civilization, from the wilderness landscape, metaphorically associated with woman and danger, is at the epicenter of a male-centered cosmogony in which God the Father commands mankind to multiply, subdue the earth, and have dominion over all living things (Gen. 1:26–28). According to this domination theology, man is separate from and above nature; and it is his right and responsibility to control, subjugate, and bend the environment according to his own greater human purposes and needs.

Thus, throughout antiquity, the building of cities and towns was a sacred religious act that separated man from the world of nature, reflected the imposition of his will on the natural order, and fulfilled his earthly destiny as God's agent. Early cities were founded by priests, kings, and heroes as the locus of creation and the symbolic center of the universe. The wilderness that lay outside the security of city walls was personified as female, profane, and savage.[25]

This ancient dichotomy continued to structure attitudes toward the environment in the "New World." The New England colonists saw themselves as "Soldiers of Christ" in a war against wilderness and "celebrated westward expansion as evidence of 'God's Blessing and God's Progress.' " "The occupation of wild territory . . . proceeds with all the solemnity of a providential ordinance," wrote William Gilpin, an early governor of Colorado and supporter of America's Manifest Destiny. As one nineteenth-century guidebook for American pioneers advertised: "You look around and whisper, 'I vanquished this wilderness and made the chaos pregnant with order and civilization. . . .' "[26]

One can easily find countless other examples of man's metaphorical impregnation of nature's "virgin soil" with the seeds of his superior civilization. Terms like "busting virgin sod," "reducing the land to fruitful subjection," "exploiting untapped resources," "harnessing nature," and "unlocking nature's secrets" remind us of man's "God-given" vanquishing power over woman, and the natural and potentially dangerous forces with which she is associated.

Popular fables, fairy tales, and folklore perpetuate this mythology by depicting the forest as dark, foreboding, sinister, and unquestionably woman's domain. Hansel and Gretel were abused by a wicked forest witch. In *The Wizard of Oz*, the Wicked Witch of the West terrorized Dorothy and her friends in the Black Forest. In the medieval forests of the Austrian Tyrol and the Bavarian Alps lived a Wild Woman of enormous size, with a hideous mouth that stretched from ear to ear and immense pendulous breasts, who stole human babies and left her own offspring in their place. The forests of Russia and Czechoslovakia are haunted by a creature with a woman's face, the body of a sow, and legs of a horse.[27]

In utopian and dystopian novels, the creation of a secure, stable, man-made environment free from the contaminating pollution of nature is a frequent theme. Take for example, the statement made by D503, the Chronicler of Eugene Zamiatin's *We* (1924): "Man ceased to be a wild animal the day he built the first wall. Man ceased to be a wild man only on the day when the Green Wall was completed, when by this wall we isolated our machinelike, perfect world from the irrational, ugly world of trees, birds and beasts."[28]

Fictive literature provides other examples. Nathaniel Hawthorne created a primeval forest around seventeenth-century Salem, Massachusetts, in his novel *The Scarlet Letter* (1850). Hawthorne's forest symbolized the moral wilderness in which the adultress Hester Prynne wandered for so long. "Pearl, her illegitimate daughter, 'imp of evil, emblem and product of sin,' is the only character at home in the wilderness."[29]

However, at the turn of the century and during the following decades, a number of realist American novels were written that challenged the universality of the male mythological cosmos by describing positive relationships between women and cities and men and the wilderness. Because novels like Hamlin Garland's *Rose of Dutcher's Cooley*

(1895), Theodore Dreiser's *Sister Carrie* (1900), Willa Cather's *'O Pioneers!* (1913), and Sinclair Lewis's *The Job* (1917) and *Main Street* (1920) treated women's life experience realistically, they offended many readers and were anything but popular at the time of their publication. Not surprisingly, the authors were influenced by the rise of the labor movement, the emergence of urban social welfare agencies, and the great second wave of feminism in America.[30]

The male heroes in these works of fiction flee from the materialistic evils of the city to the Edenic frontier—be it the forest, river, or high seas—in search of their own lost innocence and an "authentic existence." The female heroines flee from the bareness and torpor of the prairie and the small town to the freedom of the city in search of experience and adulthood. The American wilderness has a brutalizing, coarsening, and limiting effect on the lives of these women.[31]

In Cather's *'O Pioneers!*, when Alexandra's childhood friend, Carl Lindstrom, returns from years in the city complaining that he has "nothing to show for it all but the exorbitant rent that one has to pay for a few square feet of space," she responds: "I'd rather have had your freedom than my land. We pay a high rent too, though we pay differently. We grow hard and heavy here . . . and our minds get stiff. If the world were no wider than my cornfields, if there were not something besides this, I wouldn't feel that it was much worthwhile to work."[32]

In another example that foreshadows the indolence, stagnation, and isolation of contemporary suburban life for many women, Carol, who is lured into marriage to a small-town doctor in Lewis's *Main Street*, is made "timorous by the spying eyes and inertia of Gopher Prairie." She finds the ancient stale inequalities, voices a militant distrust of beauty, and views the village as "a social appendix aspiring to succeed Victorian England as the chief mediocrity of the world."[33]

These fictional women represent an impulse contrary to the dominant Adamic myths. For these "Eves," the western "paradise" is a prison that denies them intellectual and imaginative possibilities, while cities symbolize freedom, excitement, complex moral choices, and meaningful work. Although the pattern is reversed, women and men continue to inhabit and experience the spatial world in antipathetic ways.

The moral of these stories, whether fictional, mythical, or biblical, is clear. Man, by "virtue" of his birthright, is separate from, morally superior to, and sovereign over "Mother Nature," who, like woman, he may tame and exploit for his own benefit. The dichotomization of cities and wilderness is yet another cosmological construct in the symbolic universe of male supremacy.

The Territorial Imperative

These spatial dichotomies that define the dual realms of male superiority and female inferiority are protected and maintained through man's territorial dominance and control. Certainly both women and men exhibit territorial behavior; however, their motives for claiming space and defending spatial boundaries are very different.

Whether consciously or not, every day each of us claims, demarcates, and defends geographic space—from saving seats in theaters and lunchrooms by protecting them with sweaters, coats, and books, to assuming that family members will sit in the same seats at the dinner table each night. We build fences and plant hedges along the boundaries that separate our own property from our neighbors'; and we lock our doors and install burglar alarms to defend our homes against intruders. On a more public scale, municipal and state governments post official "welcome" signs to inform travelers when they have "entered" and "left" their respective jurisdictions; and federal governments establish passports, immigration quotas, and international agreements over air and water rights designed to control who may cross a nation's boundaries and for what duration and purpose they may occupy that country's space.

Why is this territorial behavior so prevalent and seemingly essential? Territories manage personal identity by establishing the spatial and psychological boundary between self and other, whether the self is an individual or group. When we are unable to control our own territory, our identity, sense of well-being, self-esteem, and ability to function may become seriously impaired. For this reason, uninvited territorial intrusions are a serious matter and can lead to strong defensive actions.[34] The invasion of a person's privacy by a talkative stranger in an adjacent airplane seat may be met with annoyance, rude indifference, or stony silence; the invasion of a "white" neighborhood by a black family with acts of vandalism against the "invaders'" property; and the invasion of one country by another with killing and bloodshed.

Secondly, territorial behavior is important because we learn to judge ourselves and each other according to how well we are able to establish and maintain our self/other boundaries. People who are "centered" in their identity are not "thrown off balance" by others, or by their surroundings. Those who know and assert their own "limits" are admired, although at times reluctantly, since such behavior can threaten those who are less self-assured. (The statement "No thank you, I don't drink" is often met with "Oh, come on! Have just a little

one with me. I don't like to drink alone.") Further, we also make judgments about people according to their "belonging" to established territories. Those who have "settled down" in a home of their own are
viewed as stable, trustworthy members of the community, while
homeless vagrants are subject to arrest and fine.

We learn at an early age that social status and power are closely
linked to spatial dominance. Youngsters scare themselves half to
death by daring each other to trespass on a stranger's property without getting caught. Such territorial aggression is highly regarded by
peers. Children playing "capture the flag" and football discover that
the "winners" in society are those who are best able to "conquer"
space, invade and acquire someone else's, and defend their own. But
not all children who grow up in a patriarchal society learn the same
territorial lessons, and for "good" reason. Little boys are socialized to
become the men who will continue to safeguard male supremacy; little girls are socialized to become the women who will support them.

Boys are raised in our society to be spatially dominant. They are
encouraged to be adventurous, to discover and explore their surroundings, and to experience a wide range of environmental
settings.[35] They learn how to claim more space than girls through
their body posture (boys' arms and legs spill over the sides of chairs
while girls sit in restrained "ladylike" positions); verbal assertiveness
(boys are taught to speak up, girls to be diffident); and superior social
status (males in the family have much greater access to automobiles
than do females, be they teenagers or adults).

Girls are raised in our society to expect and accept spatial limitations. From early childhood their spatial range is restricted to the
"protected" and homogeneous environment of the home and immediate neighborhood. They are taught to occupy but not to control
space. As a result, many adult women are anxious about traveling
alone, especially to new places—afraid that if they do so they will be
harmed or get lost or both. Further, girls learn to keep their self/other
boundaries permeable so that as adults they will be able to tolerate
frequent interruptions by their children and husbands at home and
by their male coworkers and bosses in the marketplace.

Territorial behavior is intended to put and keep people in their
literal and figurative social places. It is, as Robert Sack explains, "the
social complexity, inequality, and the need for control of one
group by another which make the territorial definition of society
essential. . . ."[36]

Since antiquity, patriarchal religious rituals have been used to
maintain scrupulously the integrity of boundaries that spatially and

socially separate one group or person from another. The Roman deity Terminus, for instance, guarded boundaries. Throughout the Roman Empire, Termini stones separated the fields and defined ownership. Those who moved or overturned these stones violated both religious and civil law and could be burned alive as punishment.[37] The head of a Roman household "preserved the borders of his domain by circumambulating his fields, singing hymns, and driving sacrificial victims before him."[38]

In fifteenth- and sixteenth-century Britain, annual Rogationtide ceremonies (later called perambulation ceremonies) required the parish priest to lead a lengthy procession around the village as he "beat the bounds," striking certain markers with a stick to point out the boundaries of the community. Appropriate prayers, religious utterances, and biblical readings were included, such as, "Cursed be he that removes his neighbor's landmark" (Deut. 27:17). Children's heads were deliberately bumped against trees and markers to make sure they remembered important boundary distinctions. In modern times, the creation of land surveys, maps, and legal documents such as property deeds have replaced perambulation; but remnants of pagan and medieval religious boundary customs remain in our annual Halloween ceremonies. The jack o'lantern was originally "the ghost of a long-ago remover of landmarks forever doomed to haunt boundary lines."[39]

Through the legacy of these long-forgotten religious practices, designed to reinforce the territorial definition of patriarchal society, we have been led to believe that preserving and defending the boundaries of our homes and homeland against "outsiders" is a sacred moral obligation; and that giving our lives in order to do so is not only acceptable, it is noble. The very word "patriotism" can evoke "religious fervor," as well it should, for like the maintenance of territorial boundaries, the origins of national allegiance are also theological. The first ancient cities were built as religious ceremonial centers. The shrine, palace, temple, and astronomical observatory were all tied to gods and goddesses and to the ritual secrets of the priesthood— magic, prophecies, and sacred messages written in the stars. "Conquerers did not raze a city to the ground simply out of wanton fury," writes Yi-Fu Tuan, "in such destruction they appropriated a people's gods by rendering them homeless, and in appropriating the gods, the conquerers acquired a civilization."[40]

Historically, men have erected public altars for patriotic worship and monuments to memorialize departed warriors and apostles of sacrifice. During the French Revolution, for instance, the Legislative

Assembly decreed that each commune raise an "altar to the Fatherland."[41] Today every modern nation-state continues to enshrine its nationalism in "sacred" architectural landmarks. America, for example, has the Statue of Liberty, the Washington Monument, and Independence Hall.

A second, equally important historical mechanism used to evoke intense feelings of protection and loyalty toward one's nation is the association of the "body politic" with mother and motherhood. Plato, for instance, boldly proposed to Socrates that "they were formed and fed in the womb of the earth," that their country was "their mother and also their nurse," and that her citizens, "as children of the earth and their own brothers," were obligated "to defend her against attack."[42]

The national flag also serves as a symbolic vehicle for transferring the personal love, protection, and loyalty we associate with our homes and mothers—an almost singular image in the human imagination— to the abstract political idea of the nation-state. For example, during the American Civil War it became customary to display the flag on or near each home. Samuel Osgood, a minister, wrote in "The Home and Flag," an article published in *Harper's New Monthly Magazine* in 1863, "What sight could become more expressive than the good mother seated at the window . . . from which floats the household flag."[43]

The amorphous, impersonal nation-state is thus transformed into a personalized motherland/homeland in the embodiment of the national flag. Defending the flag is tantamount to defending your mother and the house in which she raised you. Here is how one American soldier expressed it during World War II: "I am fighting for that big white house . . . where my brother and I spent so many happy and never-to-be-forgotten hours. . . . I am fighting for those two gray-haired grownups who live in that house right now. . . . I am fighting for my home and your home, my town and your town . . . that American belief . . . in an almighty God. . . . We cannot lose."[44]

Such impassioned, "religiously motivated" nationalism is generally highly commended in every country; for in defending your own "sacred soil," you are also defending the actual personality of your culture, its "way of life," its people. Battles over geographic space are essential to the maintenance of a patriarchal world view in which one group sees itself as superior and all others inferior; one must dominate, the other capitulate; one must win, the other lose.

The history of patriarchal civilization is chronicled through episodes of "holy" war and epochs of imperialistic conquest—Rome's in

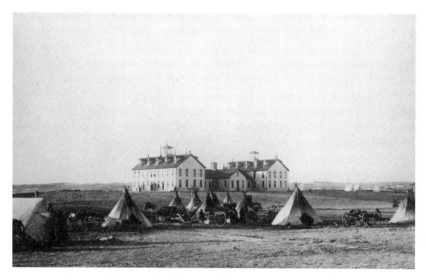

Figure 4. Indians camp near a boarding school on the Pine Ridge Agency in South Dakota, 1891. In the late 1800s the government established boarding schools to inculcate Indian children with the values of the white world. Ideally, the government sought to locate these schools far away from the "vicious and idle influence" of the reservation. Indian families not infrequently camped in the fields adjacent to the school campuses in order to be close to their children. Photograph courtesy the Western History Collections, University of Oklahoma Library.

the first century, Britain's in the nineteenth century, Germany's in the twentieth century. Men have been taught that, as the superior group in society, they are morally obligated to "protect" the integrity of both their country and "their" women through social domination and physical strength, be it nuclear power or muscle power, and for the same reason: to assert control over the boundaries of both nationhood and personhood.

Gender and Spatial Ability

Does this patriarchal socialization result in different spatial abilities and perceptions for women and men? Is there a dichotomy in the way women and men structure space? And if so, are biologically different sexual anatomies or socially different gender roles the cause? The classic argument for the former was made by psychologist Erik Erikson, who in 1937 began his controversial work on the body origins of children's play and its related spatial expression, and summarized his research in *Childhood and Society* (1965) in a section entitled "Genital Modes and Spatial Modalities." Succinctly put, he concluded that girls build enclosures with low walls and elaborate doorways which mimic the womb and are "expressly peaceful" and boys build vertical towers or walls with "cannonlike protrusions" which mimic the penis, in which "there is . . . much play with the danger of collapse or downfall. . . . ruins were exclusively boys' constructions."[45]

Erikson's explanation for the seemingly different ways that girls and boys structure space understandably caused derisive reactions. Feminist critics pointed out that the "biology as destiny" theory which his work seemed to support has been effectively used throughout history to explain and justify sexism, racism, and classism. Further, Erikson failed to account adequately for the overriding effects of socialization through which girls are taught to relate to personal body space, interiors, and the domestic sphere and boys to reflect upon public, outdoor space.

More recent research on spatial ability demonstrates that at early ages females score lower than boys on tests of spatial organization (the perception of objects in space) and spatial visualization, or imagining the movement of objects in space.[46] Researchers admit that the causes for these sex differences in spatial ability are still unclear. Yet the data have been used by some to account for the fact that there are "naturally" more men than women in "spatial professions" like architecture, engineering, urban design, and geography. Further, these theoreticians conclude that eliminating social discrimination would not eliminate this tendency since the causes are related to inherent biological differences in women and men.[47] Of course no one has suggested that since boys develop language skills later than do girls, they should avoid professions that rely heavily upon the use of language.

In evaluating men's and women's spatial "abilities," it is important to remember that test scores are valid only for average individuals among large populations; that there is always wide variation above and below the means for both sexes; and that even if on average boys are better at solving spatial problems than girls, vast numbers of girls score higher than an equally vast number of boys. Further, there is no evidence linking success in the spatial professions with test scores in spatial ability.[48]

In a society where parents have traditionally given their little boys "erector" sets and building blocks to play with and their little girls dolls, is biology or society responsible for gender differences in spatial form and perception? We simply do not know. Until we do, it seems to me our energies would be best directed toward eliminating social barriers that discourage women from becoming architects and engineers.

Are there differences in the way women and men who become architects design space? Insofar as each brings different social identities to their work, I believe there are. My point of view is shared by others and is not a new one. Henry Atherton Frost, the man responsible for founding and running the first professional architecture school for women in America, the Cambridge School of Architecture and Landscape Architecture (1917–42), wrote in 1941: "The woman architect is interested in housing rather than houses, in community centers for the masses rather than in neighborhood clubs for the elect, in regional planning more than in estate planning, in social aspects of the profession more than private commissions. . . . Her interest in her profession embraces its social and human implications."[49]

The origin of this characterization is anchored in the different ways women and men develop psychologically and morally. Many psychological theories explain that male gender identity is critically tied to separation from the mother, while female gender identity depends upon a continuing identification with the mother. Masculinity is thus defined through separation and femininity through attachment. For men, individuality, self-expression, and noninterference with the rights of others become essential to integrity. For women, who are encouraged to sustain relationships, integrity depends upon cooperation and a consideration of other people's needs and points of view in their own judgments and decisions.[50]

Gender, Architecture, and Social Values

In architecture these different frames of reference for women and men are not necessarily manifest in the use of different spatial forms and building technologies, but rather in the different social and ethical contexts in which women and men are likely to conceptualize and design buildings and spaces. These differences were eloquently described by the English architect Eileen Gray. In an interview in Paris in 1929, she discussed the "new" modern architecture with which her male contemporaries—masters of the Modern movement like Walter Gropius, Le Corbusier, and Ludwig Mies van der Rohe—were obsessed:

This intellectual coldness which we have arrived at and which inter-
prets only too well the hard laws of modern machinery can only be a
temporary phenomenon. . . . I want to develop these formulas and
push them to the point at which they are in contact with life. . . . The
avant-garde is intoxicated by the machine aesthetic. . . . But the machine aesthetic is not everything. . . . Their intense intellectualism
wants to suppress that which is marvelous in life . . . as their concern
with a misunderstood hygiene makes hygiene unbearable. Their desire
for rigid precision makes them neglect the beauty of all these forms:
discs, cylinders, lines which undulate or zigzag, elliptical lines which are
like straight lines in movement. Their architecture is without soul.[51]

The engineering aesthetic of the Modern movement that Gray
criticized was based on the abstract, intellectual purity of rational,
geometric forms and mass-produced industrial technology. The glass-
box buildings of the new International style were stripped of all applied building decoration to "express" or reveal their inner structure
and machine-made parts. This style was seen as morally superior to
anything before it, was equated with "universal truth and beauty," and
was exported to every corner of the world regardless of climate or
culture.

Gray was ahead of her time in predicting the ultimate demise of
this noncontextual and often sterile architecture. In *From Bauhaus to
Our House* (1981) Tom Wolfe wrote, "Without a blush they [architects]
will tell you that modern architecture is exhausted, finished. They
themselves joke about the glass boxes."[52] Yet Eileen Gray's work, designed in the same understated elegance of the Modern movement
and using the same materials and architectural forms, expresses an
exceptional sensitivity to human comfort, the movement of the body,
and the activities of daily life.

Both the objects and spaces Gray designed are multipurpose and
transformable over time. In the Roquebrune house, for example (see
fig. 5), she outfitted both the master and guest bedrooms with desks
and sinks. In order to accommodate several visitors in the small house
without losing privacy, she incorporated a sectional bed/alcove in the
living room which is visually hidden by a fireplace, can be used as a
double or twin beds at night, as an extra couch by day, and includes
storage compartments for clothes and pillows. She was one of the
first, if not the first, to design colored bed-sheets, arguing that the
unmade bed could still provide beauty and color in a room.

Every detail of her work is carefully attuned to comfort the human
senses: cork table tops eliminate the clanging sound of glass on hard
surfaces; layers of soft cushions and fur throws on beds stimulate the

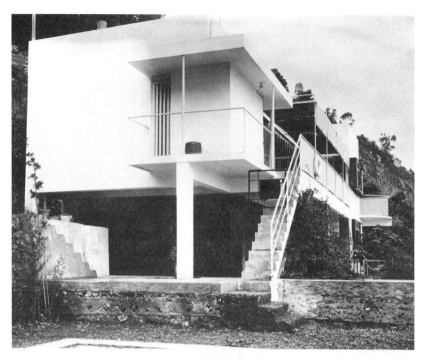

Figure 5. Gray-Badovici House, Roquebrune, Côte d'Azur, France, 1926–29, Eileen Gray, architect. View of exterior facing the sea. Photograph courtesy the Museum of Modern Art, New York.

sense of touch; an outdoor summer kitchen rids the house of food odors. Her use of three types of windows—sliding and folding, pivoting, and double-hung—combined with movable shutters, louvers, and canvas awnings allow light, air, and temperature to be modulated finely and subtly during different seasons of the year.[53]

Eileen Gray once said, "I always loved architecture more than anything else, but I did not think myself capable of it." Yet she designed her first house in her mid-forties, with no formal architectural education or apprenticeship. When she died in 1976 at ninety-seven, her furniture, architecture, and interior design stood among the most outstanding bodies of work of the Modern movement.[54]

In America, the Modern movement began to take off in the early 1950s; and it was the articulate, literate voice of another woman, Sibyl Moholy-Nagy, that criticized its architectural formulations when most believed its practitioners could do no wrong. Moholy-Nagy was an actress, writer, filmmaker, architectural historian, and teacher. In 1951 she pointed out that Mies van der Rohe's apartments were uniformly monotonous, the bathrooms and kitchens lacked privacy, light, and air, the living rooms faced each other, and the dining room bays were impassable.

Two years after the glass skyscraper Lever House was built in 1952 in New York City, Moholy-Nagy wrote, in opposition to dozens of accolades in architectural journals, "The boredom of the skyscraper box, hardly relieved by aluminum, and the gaunt ugliness of the residential matchbox, still drive the emotionally unsatisfied masses to the appliqué of true Williamsburg Baroque."[55] In her writing she excoriated the architecture of the Modern movement for its preciousness, academism, and lack of social consciousness.

Whether women design buildings or evaluate them, it seems they often tend to apply different values and concerns to architecture from those of men. We do not know the extent to which the reasons are biological or social. But this question raises many others. Why does the human body, be it woman's or man's, apparently dictate spatial language? Do we create visual form in our own body image? If we could conceptualize the body as a continuum instead of a dichotomy, would we structure space differently? If the notions of masculinity and femininity and the inequalities associated with them were abolished, how would we design and experience cities and suburbs, workplaces and dwellings? If women and men did not occupy and control space differently, what would replace the territorial boundaries that currently define our social and physical world?

These questions are complex. Some of the answers await the evolution of a greater collective self-knowledge and deeper insight into the processes of history and culture than current psychological, phenomenological, feminist, and architectural theories offer. Other, less elusive answers are suggested in the chapters that follow. Irrespective of the extent to which these questions are answerable, in asking them we move toward the realization of a very different symbolic universe.

NOTES

1. Edward T. Hall, an anthropologist, catalogued almost five thousand terms that refer to space in the *Pocket Oxford Dictionary*, almost 20 percent of all the words listed. Edward T. Hall, *The Hidden Dimension* (Garden City, N.Y.: Anchor Books, 1969), 93.

2. Shirley Ardener, "Ground Rules and Social Maps for Women: An Introduction," in *Women and Space*, 11; and Robert David Sack, *Conceptions of Space in Social Thought* (Minneapolis: University of Minnesota Press, 1980), 4.

3. Yi-Fu Tuan, *Topophilia* (Englewood Cliffs, N.J.: Prentice Hall, 1974), 61.

4. Peter L. Berger and Thomas Luckman, *The Social Construction of Reality* (Garden City, N.Y.: Anchor Books, 1967), 97–99.

5. Sack, *Conceptions of Space*, 153.

6. Lidia Sciama, "The Problem of Privacy in Mediterranean Anthropology," in *Women and Space*, ed. Ardener, 91.

7. Tuan, *Topophilia*, 21.

8. Quoted in Susan Saegert, "Masculine Cities and Feminine Suburbs: Polarized Ideas, Contradictory Realities," *Signs*, supplement, vol. 5, no. 3, (Spring 1980): 97.

9. Quoted in Sciama, "Problem of Privacy," 91.

10. Gary Zukav, *The Dancing Wu Li Masters* (New York: Bantam Books, 1979), 39–40.

11. Yi-Fu Tuan, *Space and Place* (Minneapolis: University of Minnesota Press, 1977), 43.

12. Tuan, *Space and Place*, 40, 44.

13. Dolores Hayden, "Skyscraper Seduction, Skyscraper Rape," *Heresies* 2 (May 1977): 111.

14. Tuan, *Topophilia*, 141–48.

15. Ibid., 169.

16. Tuan, *Space and Place*, 40.

17. Roderick Nash, *Wilderness and the American Mind* (New Haven: Yale University Press, 1979), 35.

18. Mazey and Lee, *Her Space*, 58.

19. Lewis Mumford, *The City in History* (New York: Harcourt, Brace, and World, 1961), 12–13.

20. Ibid., 25–27.

21. Oliver Marc, *The Psychology of the House* (London: Thames and Hudson, 1977), 12–14, 55–56, as quoted by Jane McGroarty, "Metaphors for House and Home," *Centerpoint* (Fall/Spring 1980): 182–83.

22. McGroarty, "Metaphors for House," 183.

23. Carl Jung, *Memories, Dreams and Reflections* (London: Collins, The Fontana Library Series, 1969), 250.

24. Henri Basco, *Malicroix*, as translated and quoted by Gaston Bachelard, *The Poetics of Space* (Boston: Beacon Press, 1969), 45.

25. Burton Pike, *The Image of the City in Modern Literature* (Princeton: Princeton University Press, 1981), 4–5.

26. Nash, *Wilderness*, 37, 41, 42.

27. Ibid., 12, 13.

28. Eugene Zamiatin, *We* (New York: Dutton, 1924), 88–89.

29. Quoted in Nash, *Wilderness*, 40.

30. Annette Larson Benert, "Women and the City: An Anti-Pastoral Motif in American Fiction," *Centerpoint, A Journal of Interdisciplinary Studies* 3, no. 3/4, issue 11 (Fall/Spring 1980): 151.

31. Ibid., 153.

32. Ibid., 152.

33. Ibid., 155.

34. Irwin Altman and Martin M. Chemers, *Culture and Environment* (Monterey: Brooks/Cole, 1980), 129, 130, 137.

35. Susan Saegert and Roger Hart, "The Development of Environmental Competence in Girls and Boys," Paper Series No. 78-1, Environmental Psychology Program (New York: The Graduate School and University Center of the City University of New York), 20, 21, 25. This paper also appears in *Play: Anthropological Perspectives*, ed. Michael Salter (Cornwall, N.Y.: Leisure Press, 1978).

36. Sack, *Conceptions of Space*, 181.

37. Altman and Chemers, *Culture and Environment*, 138.

38. Tuan, *Space and Place*, 166.

39. Altman and Chemers, *Culture and Environment*, 138, 139.

40. Tuan, *Space and Place*, 150–51.

41. Ibid., 177

42. Sack, *Conceptions of Space*, 187.

43. Quoted in David P. Handlin, *The American Home: Architecture and Society, 1815–1915* (Boston: Little, Brown, 1979), 86.

44. Sgt. Thomas N. Pappas, U.S. Army, "What I Am Fighting For," *Saturday Evening Post*, 10 July 1943, 29.

45. Erik H. Erikson, "Inner and Outer Space: Reflections on Womanhood," *Daedalus* 93, no. 2 (Spring 1964): 590–91.

46. Mazey and Lee, *Her Space*, 77.

47. Ibid., 9.

48. Ibid., 50.

49. Mary Otis Stevens, "Struggle for Place: Women in Architecture, 1920–1960," in *Women in American Architecture*, ed. Torre, 91–95.

50. Carol Gilligan, *In a Different Voice* (Cambridge: Harvard University Press, 1982), 8, 16–17, 19.

51. Excerpted from "De l'Eclectisme au Doute," *L'Architecture Vivante* (1929), 17–21, as translated by Deborah F. Nevins in "From Eclecticism to Doubt," *Heresies*, issue 11, vol. 3, no. 3 (1981): 71–72.

52. Tom Wolfe, *From Bauhaus to Our House* (New York: Pocket Books, 1981), 8.

53. Deborah F. Nevins, "Eileen Gray," *Heresies*, issue 11, vol. 3, no. 3 (1981): 68–71.

54. Ibid., 68.

55. Suzanne Stephens, "Voices of Consequences: Four Architectural Critics," in *Women in Architecture*, ed. Torre, 140–41.

2

Public Architecture and
Social Status

Just as women and men have different relationships to domestic space based on their differently valued gender roles and the social power attached to each, the same is true for the public buildings that house the workings of society. Men control and occupy the houses of government, the houses of God, and the houses of commerce; and within "men's houses," women are either completely excluded or relegated to a space for listening where they cannot see or be seen. For example, in the 1800s, English women wishing to listen to the political debates conducted in the old House of Commons were expected to remain hidden in the roof-space, peering down through the central ventilators in the ceiling.[1]

Women in Orthodox Jewish synagogues still listen in silence from behind a curtain, from a separate room, or from an upper gallery to the religious services men conduct among themselves. Catholic women, including nuns, were traditionally excluded from the church sanctuary—the altar from which the priests say mass and dispense the mystical "body and blood" of Christ—but altar boys, male readers and deacons have always entered the sanctuary freely as celebrants. Women entered only after the completion of religious services, and only in order to clean up.

Public buildings that spatially segregate or exclude certain groups, or relegate them to spaces in which they are either invisible or visibly subordinate, are the direct result of a comprehensive system of social oppression, not the consequences of failed architecture or prejudiced architects. However, our collective failure to notice and acknowledge how buildings are designed and used to support the social purposes they are meant to serve—including the maintenance of social inequality—guarantees that we will never do anything to change discriminatory design. When such an awareness does exist, discrimination can be redressed. For example, several years ago, Elizabeth

Taylor's testimony to Congress about the humiliation women face having to pay to use public toilets led to legislation outlawing such facilities.[2]

More recently, in a 1990 court case, a Houston, Texas, woman was unanimously acquitted by a jury of four women and two men for using a men's restroom in desperation at a country-western concert. The woman, Denise Wells, had been waiting in an endlessly long queue to the women's room when she saw a man escort his date into the men's room across the way, where there was no line. "I just followed them in," she explained.[3]

Wells and the other woman were ejected from the concert by a police officer and fined $200 each for violating a 1972 municipal ordinance that makes it unlawful "for any person to knowingly and intentionally enter any public restroom designated for the exclusive use of the sex opposite to such person's sex . . . in a manner calculated to cause a disturbance."[4] Wells maintained that she did not enter the men's room in any such manner. "I was embarrassed to death," she said.[5] A male witness testified that Wells covered her eyes with her hands and apologized profusely. "She didn't mean to cause any disturbance," he said. "I felt real sorry for her."[6]

In Houston, as in virtually all other cities in the United States, plumbing codes for public buildings have long called for a higher combined number of toilets and urinals in men's rooms than toilets in women's rooms. The assumption was that more men than women attended sporting events and conventions. In 1985, the Houston code was changed after studies found that this assumption was not correct and that women, by dint of biology, needed more sanitary facilities than an equal number of men.[7]

But Denise Wells happened to be at the Summit, a seventeen-thousand-seat auditorium built in 1975.[8] Her case drew national attention. Hundreds of women wrote to her offering to pay her ticket. Her lawyer, Valorie Wells Davenport (who is also her sister), commented, "This has struck a chord with women across the country. We've heard from women in Australia, Canada, all in support. . . . You'd think the men's room should be the last bastion, but there's an inequality of space for women."[9] One of the jurors, Freida Felton, succinctly summarized the significance of the case: "I think women's needs have been ignored for too long. It's time we go back to public buildings and provide adequate facilities for women."[10]

To be consciously aware of the social dimensions of architecture enables all of us, including architects, to evaluate and transform existing buildings more successfully and to propose other, more inclusive solutions. Separate entries in public schools for boys and girls, separate sections in restaurants for blacks and whites, the absence of curb-cuts and ramps for wheelchairs in most public buildings except hospitals are all now virtually illegal because of the actions of those whose commitment to social equality was informed by a spatial consciousness.

In the last chapter, two precepts that structure the patriarchal symbolic universe were introduced: dichotomy and territoriality. In this chapter, they reappear in four distinctly different public buildings: the office tower; the department store and its contemporary version, the shopping mall; and the maternity hospital. Though each building type differs in visual appearance and is designed for different human activities, they all institutionalize and transmit the privileges and penalties of social caste. Analyzing their separate architectural histories and formal designs in juxtaposition one to the other exposes a recurrent pattern in the hierarchical claiming, use, and control of space within each physical setting. These territorial patterns are based on the familiar inequalities of gender, race, and class distinctions—in these examples among bosses and employees; merchants, clerks, and customers; doctors, nurses, midwives, and patients. Spatial dichotomies exist in notions of urban/suburban existence associated with department stores and shopping malls, and in the schism between the public workplace/private dwelling in arguments over the hospital versus the home or "homelike" birth center as the "best" place in which to give birth. A third pattern—the importance of the profit motive—will become apparent as a central theme in the orgins, evolution, and cultural meaning of all four environments. Recognizing these commonalities as socially constructed underlays in the histories and uses of different kinds of public buildings enhances our understanding of the landscape of our daily lives and the nature of the community life it shapes.

The Office Tower: Cathedral of Commerce

The skyscraper was made technologically possible as a building type through the development of steel frame construction in the 1860s and the invention of the elevator. But its social origins are found in a real estate market in which building costs were far less important than the cost of urban land. Further, the repetitive, anonymous office spaces in the tall building could suitably accommodate, through its economy of scale, the hundreds of low-status clerical workers needed to operate the new white-collar enterprises, such as mail-order houses and insurance companies, that arose at the turn of the century.

Organized according to popular principles of scientific management which viewed workers as units of production, interior spaces
were designed to break down the work process into a series of discrete
tasks and transactions between departments to coordinate the flow of
paper. Louis Sullivan, aptly called the "father of the skyscraper," described the result in his treatise *Kindergarten Chats* (1896): "An indef-
inite number of stories of offices piled tier upon tier, one tier just like
another tier, one office just like all the other offices—an office being
similar to a cell in a honey-comb, merely a compartment, nothing
more."[11]

In direct contrast, the "open office landscape" developed as part of
the 1950s management consultancy movement as a status-free form
of layout ostensibly to promote human relations through increased
interaction, direct communication, and a decentralization of power
among workers and managers. In reality the plan allowed workers to
be interrupted constantly; it destroyed their ability to concentrate and
placed them under the relentless surveillance of supervisors and coworkers. Most often, those who still work under such conditions are
women: "The NBC Spot Sales Department has sixteen male salesmen
and sixteen female sales assistants. The salesmen hustle television
spots (sixty- thirty- and ten-second commercial breaks) to advertisers.
They sit in individual windowed offices. The women are crowded (all
sixteen of them) onto the outer-office floor. The noise of sixteen
typewriters, telephones, and voices on that outer floor is almost
deafening."[12]

Spatial privacy is an excellent index for measuring social status.
The executive's "inner sanctum" is buffered by the receptionist's
lobby, the stenographers' pool, and the personal secretaries' office, all
of which safeguard the boss's privacy and the impressive and arcane
power he or she represents. While protocol requires employees to ask
permission to enter their bosses' office, a boss can walk freely into a
subordinate's office or desk area at any time.

Similarly, the assignment of valuable light and space is related to
one's gender-based occupational status. In repetitive skyscraper
floorplans, interior fluorescent-lit space is invariably allocated to clerical workers (predominantly women), exterior offices with natural
light and views to executives (predominantly men). In the John Hancock Building in Boston, a senior vice-president is allowed 406 square
feet of space compared to a clerical worker's 55.[13] In the *Secretarial
Ghetto* (1972), Mary Kathleen Benet showed that women receive the
same proportion of office space as they do pay, 20 to 50 percent less
than men doing the same work in the same office.[14]

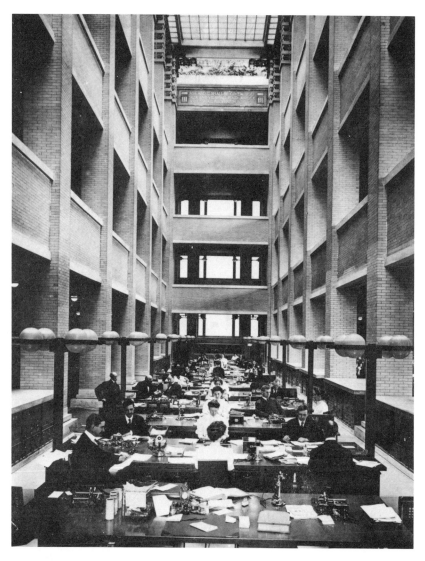

Figure 6. Larkin Company Administration Building, Buffalo, New York, 1904, Frank Lloyd Wright, architect. The interior layout was designed to enforce the regimented, hierarchical, sexually segregated work force. Note the supervisor on the left who is able to see all in this "open landscape" office design, which is advanced for the date. Photograph courtesy the Museum of Modern Art, New York.

Gender, race, class, occupation, and other factors like age and disability collectively create distinctly different spatial experiences for people, even within the same environmental setting (see chapter 1). In office towers, the hidden architectural realm of the blue-collar maintenance worker—with its fire stairs, boiler room, storage rooms, janitor's closets, loading docks, and below-ground entries—is rarely seen by white-collar workers and the general public who enter the building's formal, marble-clad lobby and ascend to their destinations in richly paneled elevators.

While interior space in office towers reflects and reinforces a hierarchy of social status among workers and bosses, the height of such buildings symbolizes a hierarchy of status among the "corporate giants" who build and own them. When John Jacob Raskob, a vice-president of General Motors, started building the Empire State Building in New York (completed in 1931), he worried that his competitor Walter Chrysler would outdo him. Hamilton Weber, the original rental manager of the Empire State Building, recalled: "John J. finally reached into a drawer and pulled out one of those big fat pencils schoolchildren liked to use. He held it up and said to Bill Lamb [his architect], 'Bill, how high can you make it so it won't fall down?' "[15] The result was a 102-story, 1,250-foot-tall building with 7 miles of elevator shafts and enough floor space to shelter a city of 80,000 people. In the process of construction 14 workers' lives were lost.[16]

The competition for height and the pressure by developers to build quickly to realize a profit took precedent over safety standards for workers. The daredevil ironworkers who erected the structural steel, nicknamed "sky-boys," took the greatest risks. During the Depression, those who were unemployed often hung around job sites to take the place instantly of any man who fell. In 1930, *Fortune* magazine noted that a "bloodless building" was a "marvel"; it was estimated that from three to eight deaths occurred on a sizable building site. Today, even though workers' unions have significantly improved safety standards, approximately one worker out of fifteen dies within ten years of entering the trade.[17]

Despite the high cost of human life, the skyscraper race has not stopped. In 1969, the twin towers of New York's World Trade Center surpassed the height of the Empire State Building. In 1973, Sears Roebuck and Company built a 110-story tower in Chicago, designed to top the height of the World Trade Center by 100 feet because, as the Sears company explained, "Being the largest retailer in the world, we thought we should have the largest headquarters."[18] In so doing they created a 1,450-foot-tall building whose air conditioning has the capacity to cool 6,000 homes and whose electrical system is capable of serving a city of 147,000 people.[19]

The excessive height of these antihuman, environmentally irresponsible man-made mountains has been lauded by many architects as the "answer" to the future development of urban form. For example, in 1956 Frank Lloyd Wright, whose mentor and teacher had been Louis Sullivan, proposed to build a mile-high, needle-shaped "city" to house 130,000 people on Chicago's lakefront. Following in the footsteps of the "master," one of Wright's students, Paolo Soleri, has developed sketches for over thirty futuristic vertical cities that range in height from three hundred feet to one mile with an unbelievable population density of up to twelve hundred people per acre.[20] Soleri frequently uses the Empire State Building as a scale symbol in his drawings to dramatize the unimaginable size of his "visionary cities."[21]

Such "architectural machismo" is not amusing.[22] Super-towers use up an insupportable amount of energy, superheat the atmosphere, create fierce gusts of wind that explode glass plate windows and lift pedestrians off their feet, darken neighborhoods, change the ecology of local parks with their enormous shadows, and turn into death traps if fire breaks out.[23] Further, each new skyscraper brings thousands more people, cars, and taxis into already critically overcrowded and unhealthy streets and sidewalks. Nevertheless, skyscraper construction in the United States continued unabated throughout the 1980s.

Not all architects are insensitive to the urban problems that skyscrapers create. Some share Philip Johnson's belief that "There's absolutely no need for skyscrapers. They're a sheer fantasy of American bourgeoisie." Yet even Johnson's awareness has not curtailed his building activities. He explains: "The more skyscrapers I build, the more it strains the neck a bit, but it's pleasant to see them growing, like a good asparagus bed."[24]

To sum up: in the twentieth century, the economics of urban land, the invention of the elevator and steel-and-glass construction, and the egos of businessmen and the architects they employed gave rise to increasingly tall office structures designed to segregate the users spatially according to occupational and class status. In the twenty-first century, the office workplace will be shaped by the economics of energy; the scarcity of ecologically critical open land; the presence of toxic substances in building materials and sites; computer-based technologies; and an increasingly large female workforce. In the future, all toxic and carcinogenic substances, such as asbestos and radon, must be eliminated from office buildings, and health and safety standards must be developed for workers using office equipment such as video display terminals that cause excessive eyestrain, emotional stress, and exposure to radioactive emissions. The amount of energy consumed by office buildings must be significantly reduced through the application of renewable solar and hydropowered technologies, and energy-conserving design strategies for lighting, heating, cooling, and ventilating systems. Building incinerators must be designed to eliminate further pollution of the atmosphere. Zoning mandates must include rooftop, terraced, and ground-level gardens and parks to help cities breathe, reduce noise levels, and calm the human senses, and must provide on-site childcare and recreation for workers and their families. These changes in the architecture of the commercial office building are essential if we are to become a society that is environmentally and socially responsible.

The Department Store: Palace of Consumption

While the office tower symbolizes man's economic role as producer and worker, the American department store developed in the 1880s as a public meeting place where women could fulfill their economic role as "conspicuous consumers" in the burgeoning industrial order. These new palaces of consumption were designed to "dazzle, delight and seduce the customer."[25]

The architecture, which characteristically included a rotunda and galleries that opened onto a central court usually topped by an elaborate leaded glass skylight, was monumental and cathedral-like. The interiors of these early stores were plushly appointed throughout with marble floors, oriental rugs, crystal chandeliers, polished mahogany and French glass counters, and ornate fountains. At the entry to New York's Siegel and Cooper Company, shoppers were greeted by a fountain that included a figure of a Greek goddess over twenty feet high. John Wanamaker's store in Philadelphia contained a two-thousand-seat auditorium, a pipe organ with nearly three thousand pipes, a Grand Court with towering marble columns, and a Greek Hall with six thousand more seats.[26]

The department store soon became the women's equivalent to men's downtown clubs. Ladies' lunchrooms were such a successful feature that Macy's in New York City (which opened the first ladies' lunchroom in 1878) included a public restaurant for 2,500 people in its new Herald Square store in 1902.[27] The department store also provided elaborate lounges and restrooms, reading rooms, writing rooms stocked with complimentary stationery and pens, and restaurants with live musicians for the comfort and convenience of their "guests," as customers were called. However, these amenities proved to be expensive and did not result in increased sales revenue.[28]

Department store managers solved the problem of these "nonproductive" expenditures by establishing a two-class system of space. While no expense was spared on the luxurious public areas, the "behind-the-scenes" space reserved for the use of working-class employees, such as lockers, lunchrooms, and restrooms, were "typically squalid, unsanitary, and unappealing."[29]

The spatial segregation of the paying customers from those who served them was further reinforced by store policy which prohibited employees from using public facilities. The employees, however, did not cooperate. They objected to the separate employees' entrances tucked into dingy back streets, standing in marked contrast to the ceremonial portals designed for customers. Saleswomen deliberately disobeyed the rules at Filene's Department Store in Boston, which restricted them to certain elevators, and angered management by entertaining their friends in the customers' lounge and habitually walking past the public restaurant to the employees' cafeteria instead of using the prescribed backstairs route.[30]

After the turn of the century, employee facilities were generally upgraded, but the motives were strictly economic. Managers hoped that better surroundings would reduce class conflict "across the counter" and encourage saleswomen to identify with both the middle- and upper-class consumers and the goods they consumed. One writer of the time explained: "If a girl, say, reared in humble surroundings, spends some part of her day amid pictures and cheerful furniture and tasteful rugs and books and sunlight, will she not insensibly acquire a clearer insight into the ideas and needs of the majority of the store's customers? Will she not, then, be better able to wait upon her trade deftly, sympathetically, and understandingly?"[31] In other words, happy and informed workers would sell more eagerly and efficiently.

Economic considerations related to the notion of gender roles also influenced the organization and use of department store space. Managers, convinced that busy businessmen did not enjoy pushing their way through crowds of women, designated the first floor "male territory," and placed men's clothing near main entrances, adding service desks to speed their shopping. Similarly convinced that women preferred to shop in privacy and leisure, they placed women's clothing on the middle floors. Today the layout in many suburban department stores remains much the same.

The Shopping Mall:
The Signature Building of Our Age

The magnetism of the contemporary shopping mall is derived from the cultural belief that shopping can be an entertaining social experience in its own right. Like the urban department store, the suburban mall's spatial organization and visual appearance are the outcome of a merchandizing plan directed toward manipulating shoppers to maximize profits. For example, the architectural "rules" that govern mall form are designed to control pedestrian traffic by placing well-known "flagship" or "magnet" stores at opposite ends of a covered interior "street" generally no longer than 220 yards (about 200 meters), for beyond this length the continuous flow of people begins to break down into separate circuits. Mall widths are precisely planned to encourage shoppers to cross from side to side to benefit the small retail stores. Usually a zone of circulation about ten feet (three meters) wide is provided outside each shopfront, creating an "interior street" of about twenty feet (six meters) to which an additional central zone of ten feet can be added for seating, planters, and fountains at intervals to relieve the visual monotony of the uninterrupted mall perspective. Shopfronts and signs are rigidly aligned to ensure that each is clearly and equally visible to the greatest number of passing shoppers.[32]

Shopping malls are cathedral-like monuments to a new faith in consumption. In the past, when religion dominated even civic life, the churches were the most sensually satisfying social gathering places in the community. Their soaring vaulted spaces were filled with the redolence of incense, and with oratory and singing. Today, shopping malls, with their great sunlit atriums, provide equivalent theatrical public settings.

Malls are artificially controlled environments designed to create illusion and fantasy. "Outdoor cafes" are not really outdoors; there is no rain, snow, heat, or cold. Trees and plants grow from tile floors, and waterfalls cascade down carefully executed walls and terraces in syncopation with piped-in music. The Galleria, a three-tiered mall built in Houston in 1970, contains an ice skating rink, an element as exotic in the hot Texas climate as the tropical gardens that "grow" in the malls in northern cities.

The shopping mall has become a way of life. One 1985 survey showed that Americans make 7 billion trips in and out of shopping centers every year and spend more time in malls than anywhere else except home, job, or school.[33] A study of the 170 million adults who visited a mall in America in June 1989 indicated that 64 percent were women, not a surprising statistic since the average mall has five times as many women's shoe stores as it has similar stores for men. While the large numbers of women employed today suggest that a much smaller percentage would have time to shop leisurely in the relaxing surroundings of a mall, this study concludes that the mall, like its earlier counterpart, the department store, is a "woman's world."[34]

For mothers with babies in strollers, the curbfree, weatherproof, quiet mall is one of the few manageable public spaces. One such woman described what the mall means to her: "There is no need like the need of a mother alone in the house with a small child . . . for public space. I used to fantasize the ideal spaces—large rooms full of play equipment with comfortable chairs for mothers to sit and socialize, like nannies in the park. But you can't go to parks in the winter, and even in summer you aren't likely to see anyone you know. Malls—flat, controlled malls—come very close to fulfilling what is probably a vestigial need."[35]

The mall can also be an antidote to loneliness and isolation for seniors, providing them with comfortable places to sit and linger, meet each other, have a cup of coffee, and "people watch." The shopping mall is one of the few public spaces, in our age-segregated society, where older people and younger people can see each other, since they are the two groups who most regularly use the mall for social purposes. Frequently, older people can be found at malls for health reasons. The sheltered, flat mall terrain is ideal for walking, and all across the United States malls have formed "walkers' clubs" for seniors. (Many malls open their doors early for morning constitutionals.)

For suburban teenagers—too old to stay at home and too young to go to bars—shopping centers are the only public places in which to congregate, socialize, and "pick up dates." Teenagers sit in the mall instead of the public library to do their schoolwork. The "food courts" offer them an affordable alternative to the increasingly empty family dining room at home. Instead of growing up to be streetwise, these suburban children learn to be "mallwise," adjusting to the subtleties of a large-scale, controlled, artificial environment—learning the lessons of materialism that will shape their human identities and social aspirations.

The suburban mall acts as an ideal "substitute city" for the cityless by including the convenience and amenities of urban life and excluding the conditions that drove their customers out of the city. Within the protected enclosure of its windowless, interior world, there is no automobile traffic, noise, or fumes, and comparatively little crime. The malls keep out poor people by their high prices and maintain their white exclusivity by choosing not to carry products and styles that might appeal to racial and ethnic minority customers. Ironically, the suburban mall, regarded as the place most hostile to the traditional city, adapted an architectural iconography derived from urbanism—the sequence of landmarks on the landscape that characterize the medieval hill town: the defensive wall-enclosure, monumental gateways, sheltered internal streets, and "node" piazzas punctuated with fountains.

The dichotomous relationship between cities and suburbs, pedestrians and automobiles is at the center of the development of American shopping malls as a building type. From the beginning, suburban centers were designed to separate cars, which needed parking space, from pedestrians, who needed walking space. The first planned "shopping district" in the United States, called Market Square, was built in 1916 in the Chicago suburb of Lake Forest. This and other early districts such as Country Club Plaza, built in 1922 on the outskirts of Kansas City, consisted of a grouping of buildings developed and managed as a unit, with a special parking area and an exclusively pedestrian "street."

In 1931, another evolutionary step in the design of shopping centers was taken at the Highland Park Shopping Village in Dallas, were shopfronts were turned inward, away from the public street, around a special pedestrian courtyard. By the early 1950s, in response to the great suburban population boom, this form slowly began to replace the popular strip centers consisting of a line of shops along a highway with parking in front.

Shopping malls in the 1950s, such as Northland Center in suburban Detroit, designed by architect Victor Gruen, typically had one large department store anchoring one end and two parallel rows of stores facing a landscaped pedestrian area in the middle that was open to the sky. Southdale Mall in Minnesota, also designed by Gruen (1956), was the first to include two major competing department stores, a concept some considered madness. Gruen's challenge was to devise a way of separating them as equal parts of the same center. The extreme variations in Minnesota's climate provided the architect with a second challenge—baking-hot summers and bitter cold winters discouraged shoppers from walking long distances and remaining outdoors for any length of time. To solve these two problems, Gruen proposed that Southdale be completely enclosed around a central garden court that would create a dramatic vertical interior consisting of two levels visible to each other with the two department stores at opposite ends. (Gruen's solution was inspired by the nineteenth-century covered pedestrian arcades of Europe such as the Galleria Vittorio Emanuele II in Milan, whose four stories are topped by a huge glazed roof vault and a central glass cupola 160 feet high.)

Southdale was an immediate success and shopping center professionals quickly realized that people went there by the thousands not just to shop, but to stay. Further, they saw that the two department stores did not "ruin" each other; they simply brought more people to the mall and attracted numbers of other shops. Mall "synergy" became basic to shopping mall philosophy, as did the superficial duplication of Southdale's design features: complete enclosure, two levels, a central court, and comfort control. Throughout the 1960s and 1970s the standardized enclosed mall was replicated in thousands of American suburbs, from Florida to California, regardless of climate.

Although the suburban mall was created as a "secure" environment in which nothing would distract from buying as the entire focus, in recent years the enforcement of mall security has become more and more difficult. Robberies are increasing because banks are increasingly found in malls. Rapes and the abduction of children happen in malls because women and children are there. Car thefts are a particular and inevitable problem. In this regard, suburban malls have become more "citylike."

Concomitantly, urban commercial development has increasingly incorporated suburban merchandizing and architectural design concepts. For example, in the 1960s and 1970s urban department stores began to use the spatial device of a "street of shops" to lend identity and orientation to the floors of their trading operations, which had grown to be vast and confusing during the course of department store history. In New York City, in 1976, Macy's restructured its basement floor as "The Cellar," a brick-paved arcade, selling specialty items, from housewares and gourmet food to vitamins and flowers. Bloomingdale's introduced the "B'Way" (for Broadway) in which cosmetic and fashion accessory departments flanked a glittering mirrored "street" paved with black and white marble squares. The "streetscape" concept proved to be an extremely successful method of visual merchandizing that transformed the stodgy, family-oriented department store into a theatrical amusement park.

Another aberration of urban/suburban design is the urban atrium, a high-rise shopping mall that reverses the rules governing the form of the city and its streets. Whereas department stores once competed for the light, air, and frontage provided by the pedestrian street, in these skyscrapers the walls are blank, scaleless panels whose only function is to insulate the interior core. Buildings such as Citicorp and Trump Tower in New York City, Water Tower Place in Chicago, The Gallery at Market East in Philadelphia, Embarcadero Center in San Francisco, Bonaventure Center in Los Angeles, Eaton Centre in Toronto, Le Complexe des Jardins in Montreal, and the Strand Arcade and Mid-City Centre in Sydney are but a few examples of buildings designed to "flip" the city block "outside-in," creating multitiered sidewalks tucked into vertical caverns that, like their suburban counterparts, create an artificial world of quiet gardens and commercial seduction.

The selling of specialty goods in urban centers is a tradition as old as trade itself. However, the "selling" of shopping as a pure form of social entertainment is a feature peculiar to the more recent development of urban malls like Ghirardelli Square in San Francisco, Faneuil Hall in Boston, the South Street Seaport in New York City, and Harbor Place in Baltimore. The characteristics these shopping centers share are their locations in declining areas with strong and memorable physical features including proximity to a waterfront, their ability to attract large numbers of out-of-town tourists, and their reuse and conservation of old, historic buildings. But these marketing centers are not primarily the result of some deeply rooted urban imperative to preserve elements of cultural and architectural history and provide basic goods and services to urban citizens. Rather, they are a response to surplus suburban wealth.

London's Covent Garden, housed in an architecturally important building, provides a comparable example to those found in North America. The original Central Market Building, designed by Charles Fowler, opened in 1830 and consisted of three parallel buildings linked by a colonnade. Fifty years later the two courtyards between the buildings were spanned by glazed, cast-iron frame roofs to create a fully enclosed market building. In 1974, when the fruit and vegetable market was removed to Battersea, the Greater London Council began renovation of the buildings as small shops, a project completed in 1980. The success of the "new" Covent Garden Market as a tourist attraction has, as in so many North American cities, driven small local traders away and replaced indigenous basic services and businesses with luxury and impulse-sales stores.[36]

Shopping centers like these, allegedly designed to foster urban renewal, rehabilitation, and economic development, in reality destroy the social and economic structure of the community. They should not be mistaken as the spearhead of urban regeneration when they are actually outposts of the suburban economy, located in cities because of their architectural and historic ambience and relatively inexpensive site costs. They are part of the destructive forces of gentrification that merely displace the problems of the area and its lower-income residents to some other place.

Today the shopping mall has become the signature building of our age, a central hub of community life. But malls are neither cities nor suburbs, though they incorporate spatial elements of both. They are racially and economically homogeneous, culturally arid environments skillfully shaped by the hands of merchandisers to promote profits. Malls are insular fantasy worlds where the relatively well-off pursue the study and acquisition of superfluous goods as a form of entertainment, in a society in which millions are in desperate need of something to eat and a safe, warm place to sleep. The mall is the quintessential embodiment of patriarchal dichotomies.

But it need not remain so. Today suburban, exurban, and rural areas across the country are facing the rapid depletion of ecologically important open land—farms, woods, shorelines, wetlands, and meadows—through scattered-site commercial and residential construction. The shopping mall, despite its basically retail character, could act as a centralizing influence to counteract sprawling development, magnetically drawing around it an array of public spaces and buildings for cultural and civic activities—parks and gardens, apartments, offices, hotels, theaters, restaurants, health care and child care facilities—that could bring people together face to face, thereby reweaving the social fabric of suburbia that now isolates people in private cars, housing tracts, and office centers.

The Maternity Hospital:
Blueprint for Redesigning Childbirth

Like the shopping mall, department store, and commercial office tower, the history and design of the maternity hospital demonstrates how distinctions in gender, race, and class are encoded in the shape of public buildings and the social institutions that produce them. Maternity hospitals were established in the nineteenth century as urban-based charity asylums to serve the poor, the homeless, and the working class. They were usually sponsored and run by businessmen, clergy, and community leaders and functioned as institutions offering both medical treatment and social rehabilitation.

Many of the expectant mothers in maternity hospitals were the servants of wealthy families who received their own health care in the privacy of their homes or the offices of their physicians. Others were unwed mothers who were sympathetically viewed as the "victims of ignorance and urban living." The maternity hospital provided these cases with both a "simulated home delivery" and a two-month stay, one before, one after childbirth, in a "morally uplifting" environment where they would learn to be respectable women by working to keep the hospital clean.[37]

By mid-century, doctors realized that standards of modesty, which made it unthinkable to expose a woman's genitals, and fear of their patients' disapproval should these standards be violated, had seriously hampered their clinical training in midwifery. Doctors began to see the maternity hospital—filled with women in no social position to complain—as an opportunity to remedy their ignorance of the physical processes of birth. What they could learn on poor or "fallen" women in the hospital, they could use to treat respectable women at home.

In 1848 the American Medical Association was founded to establish state licensing requirements. It set standards that excluded midwives from medical practice and promoted hospital deliveries over home deliveries. Doctors sought to centralize medical care in hospitals in order to control their own work space. For example, the doctor's skill depended upon the use of instruments. While he could carry forceps and scissors from home to home, X-ray and anesthesia machines, transfusion and sterilizing equipment, and so on, were bound to the hospital. To receive specialized medical treatment, patients would have to come to the specialist's workplace.

The convenient use of time was another motive. Birth as a home-based cottage industry was time consuming. The doctor had to travel to women's homes, remain throughout labor, and compromise his authority by deferring to family wishes about interventions. The consolidation of all patient care in the hospital eliminated travel time and allowed him to offer more patients "skilled care," while leaving the provision of their personal care and comfort to other "less important" staff members like nurses, social workers, chaplains, and cleaning women.[38] The hospitalization of childbirth placed the economic and biological control over women's reproductive capacity exactly where the rising male medical establishment wanted it—with themselves.

Women knew the great risk involved in a hospital, as opposed to a home delivery. In 1840 the mortality rate from puerperal ("childbed") fever was so high in the Vienna Lying-In Hospital that women were buried two in a coffin to disguise the actual figures, but the majority of poor women had no other choice than to use hospital facilities. There were innumerable cases of women fleeing from hospitals once they got there, committing suicide rather than entering, and begging to be admitted wherever midwives predominated, since the likelihood of survival there was inevitably greater. In 1846 a Viennese physician, Ignaz Phillip Semmelweis, discovered the cause of puerperal fever; but because he correctly pointed to doctors and the hospital environment as the cause of disease, he was ridiculed, discredited, and demoted by his peers until, unable to cope, he was committed in 1865 to the Vienna Insane Asylum, where he died.[39]

Women were led to believe hospital births were safer than home births, despite the fact that infection rates in hospitals remained higher than in homes and unnecessary or improperly performed medical interventions caused infant deaths from birth injuries to increase from 40 to 50 percent between 1915 and 1929.[40] During the 1920s, manufacturers of household cleaning products who advertised in women's magazines popularized the notion that invisible household germs were the cause of contamination, infection, and sickness. Housework was "elevated" from general standards of wholesome cleanliness to a valiant sanitary crusade against the disease-carrying dust and dirt that could affect the health of family members. At the same time, hospitals began to advertise themselves as germfree, ultraclean "white gems of purity" that were surely more sanitary than the homes of even the most diligent housewives. Since concern for birth safety was justified (in 1918 the United States ranked seventeenth out of twenty nations in maternal mortality and eleventh in infant mortality), many middle-class women turned to birth specialists in hospitals who promised them the safety they sought.[41]

Hospitals also promised greater safety and painless birth through the availability of trained personnel, special emergency equipment round-the-clock, and "Twilight Sleep" (a combination of morphine, an hallucinogenic amnesiac called scopolamine, and ether or chloroform). They offered women "lying in" a comfortable place to recuperate where maids, cooks, and nurses could care for them—an experience that had become almost impossible with the disappearance of domestic servants and the support that women had found in female friends and relatives during the nineteenth century.

The new maternity hospitals and obstetrical wards built in the 1920s were designed as homelike, almost vacationlike settings. They were characterized by porches, open-air verandas, and bright, cheerful colors to produce "charming effects" and disguise the hospitals' institutional quality. Efforts were made to maximize personal privacy and individuality. Private phones, adjustable beds, "duplex window shades," and buzzers to silently call nurses were included in each room. Further "humane touches" were provided for consumers, such as separate wards for women whose babies had died and special sleeping and waiting rooms for husbands whose wives were in critical condition.[42]

Not surprisingly, a hospital birth cost a lot more than a home birth. There were few health plans that covered maternity care in the 1920s and 1930s; birth was an out-of-pocket expense. Women's magazines educated young couples on how to "make the best birth buy" in the same way they discussed the cost of appliances and other consumer products. Husbands were encouraged to believe that providing "the best" for their wives and babies—a specialist's care and the safety and comfort of the hospital—was a sound investment and a moral obligation. Poor women turned to hospital births because they had no alternative; midwives were prohibited from practice, and private doctors refused to attend them at home.[43]

By the early 1930s, 60 to 75 percent of the births in American cities took place in hospitals. Up to this time hospitals had dramatically increased in number. After that time they increased in size, becoming vast, urban institutions accommodating both clinic and private patients, divided, as always, according to class. During the 1950s, hospitals followed the more affluent population to the suburbs.[44]

If giving birth was the ultimate in femininity, controlling and supervising it was quintessentially masculine, and the obstetrician's workplace was designed accordingly. Like factories and office buildings, obstetrical units were spatially organized to operate efficiently. Specialized tasks and workers were separated in assembly-line fashion, fragmenting both the process of birth and the space in which it occurred into three "components": the labor and delivery suite, the newborn nursery, and the postpartum nursing unit (see fig. 7). Ideally, all three were located in a spatially contiguous relationship, although often they were not. (Sometimes they were even located on different floors.)

Hospital routines were developed for the convenience of the staff. Until the late 1970s, patients were moved from one part of the hospital to another according to staff schedules and the location of

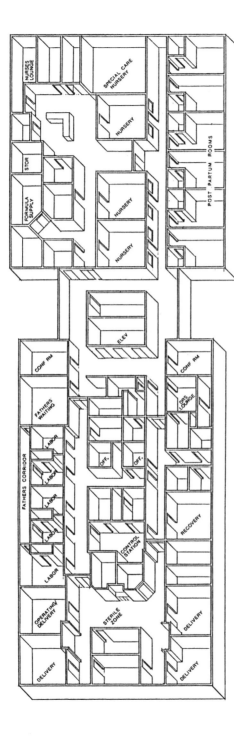

Figure 7. Axonometric drawing depicting the typical linear layout of a conventional hospital obstetrical ward. Drawing courtesy Barbara Marks, architect.

equipment. Like a product being processed in a factory, the child-bearing couple was controlled and manipulated by the hospital's rigid policies and overwhelming maze of spaces from the moment they entered the admitting office. Institutional control began with filling out depersonalized forms and the separation of the woman from her primary source of emotional support, most often her husband. Throughout the 1950s, 1960s, and 1970s, this woman's experience was not unusual: "I arrived at the hospital clutching a bath towel between my legs, dripping water. I couldn't find a wheelchair and left a trail all the way down their new, blue-carpeted hall. When I got to the labor room, they put me in a toilet area after giving me an enema. I had my first strong contraction there. I yelled for a nurse, but no one came. Another contraction came and I began doing my Lamaze slow-breathing. I finally went out into the hall and got myself a nurse. John was still filling out the forms downstairs."[45]

The maternity patient who managed to get the forms filled out before the onset of labor typically found herself confined to a wheelchair and escorted with her husband through long, anonymous corridors and elevators to the labor and delivery suite. Having arrived, they were sent their separate ways—she to labor; he to wait. Countless women told of the loneliness and fear of this experience. One recalled, "I was left alone all night in a labor room. I felt exactly like a trapped animal and I am sure I would have committed suicide if I had had the means. Never have I needed someone, anyone, as desperately as I did that night."[46] Another woman recounted, "The labor room had to be entered two by two . . . because it was too small to hold more. . . . the beds were narrow and enclosed with bars—like cribs for the insane. . . ."[47]

Hospitals lacking room often placed laboring women in a group labor room where they were further demoralized and frightened by each other's discomfort and the lack of privacy. Sometimes labor was artificially speeded up or slowed down to suit staff schedules or because a delivery room was not available at the "right" time: "When my baby was ready the delivery room wasn't. I was strapped to a table, my legs tied together, so I could 'wait' until a more convenient and 'safer' time to deliver. In the meantime, my baby's heartbeat started faltering. . . . When I regained consciousness, I was told my baby would probably not live."[48]

Having endured the labor room, when a woman was "ready" to deliver she was wheeled on a stretcher to the sterile delivery room where she was placed on a narrow metal delivery table with "stirrups" to strap her legs up high and leather thongs to tie down her arms and hands. There was no telling how long she would be there. Some women reported being strapped to the delivery table for as long as eight hours. One wrote that she was on the table for thirty-six hours, during which time her husband did not know whether she was "living or dead."[49]

Immediately following delivery the infant was whisked away from its mother to the newborn nursery for observation, while she was taken by stretcher to a recovery room. From there, she was transferred to the postpartum unit where she stayed for an average of three to five days. She saw her baby as often as hospital policy allowed and the nursing staff were able to transport it back and forth from the newborn nursery. Although some hospitals had rooming-in policies for mothers and infants, most argued against decentralized nursery care on the grounds that there was usually insufficient space in patient rooms and that it was less cost efficient because it required more staff. Other hospital policies determined who could visit the mother and infant and how often. The family was never fully united and in control of decisions until discharged from the hospital.

Between the 1950s and the 1970s, American doctors turned birth into a standardized form of industrial production in which women were, as one patient wrote, "herded like sheep through an obstetrical assembly line. . . . obstetricians today [1977] are businessmen who run baby factories."[50] During the 1970s, the idea of women gaining control over their own bodies became a major tenet of the women's movement, whose members were primarily white, educated, and middle class. Many American doctors willingly responded to feminist demands for "natural childbirth," knowing that as long as birth was hospitalized, they could define and control what "natural" meant (for example, by regularly adding routine interventions like episiotomy, forceps, Demarol, and epidural anesthesia to keep birth from taking up too much time and to allow enough "medical art" to justify their professional presence and fees).[51]

Most hospitals agreed to allow fathers in the labor and delivery rooms, other children in the mother's room, and to give mothers access to their newborns when they wanted them. Still, the hospital environment itself continued to frustrate the natural-childbirth patient by its overwhelming size, rigid bureaucratic routines, emergency equipment, and frightening desultory spaces. Only in the 1980s, when birthing rooms or "birthing suites" were added to the traditional obstetrical ward, were some childbearing couples able to experience natural childbirth in the hospital.

Patients who use hospital birthing rooms go through labor, give birth, and remain there until discharged. The atmosphere is home-like and children are made welcome; in the suites, kitchens are available for family use. The birthing rooms and suites offer couples another birth environment option—provided they are available. Since only low-risk patients can use them, a certain portion of the childbearing population is ineligible. Patients who do qualify are sometimes denied their use because they are occupied, or more often because of a combination of factors such as location and nursing staff efficiency. If the birthing room is not located directly next to the traditional labor/delivery area, the head nurse has to split the staff, sending one or more nurses to the distant birthing room. If several patients are in the labor/delivery area, as is frequently the case, the head nurse usually needs all the staff in attendance, and is forced to say no to the alternative. Further, many doctors are uncomfortable without the reassuring presence of their medical equipment and choose the traditional delivery room instead of a birthing room as a "proper place" to tend their patients. Another problem is created by the fact that birthing rooms are in hospitals, so patients using them may still receive routine pubic shaves, enemas, and labor-inducing medication, or be quickly transferred to traditional delivery rooms. With the use of medical intervention, a birthing room becomes a cosmetic change, not a real change in consumer control over childbearing. The net result is that most birthing rooms sat unused throughout the 1980s.

In summation, until the mid-nineteenth century, childbirth was a uniquely female experience that took place at home; the laboring woman was in the company of women friends and relatives, and under the guidance of an experienced midwife who patiently allowed nature to take its course without interference. The establishment of maternity hospitals rendered home birth and women's practice of midwifery illegal and "dangerous," and transformed childbearing from a normal biological event to a pathological condition requiring the kind of preventive "protection" from itself that only physicians were qualified to provide in the "safety" of hospitals. The majority of poor women in need of obstetrical help had no alternative but to use the wards in public hospitals, where in turn they were used by doctors as subjects for teaching and experimentation. The majority of affluent women were led to believe that giving birth in a luxurious private "guest room" in the lying-in hospital would guarantee a "modern," painless, safe experience and enhance their social status. Thus maternity hospitals created and enforced spatial segregation among patients of different classes and the doctors' economic and psychological monopoly over childbirth. Like the "captains of industry" who had established their own power and prestige by removing "work" from the home and relocating it in the factory and office building, doctors became a powerful elite as birth was removed from the home and institutionalized in the hospital.

Birth Centers:
Restoring Women's Birth Rights

In marked contrast to the maternity hospital is the freestanding birth center. There were 100 of them in the United States in 1983. By 1984, 300 more were planned across the country; but during that same year, soaring rates for liability insurance for maternity care put the plans on hold. In 1989 the National Association of Childbearing Centers reported that 130 birth centers were in operation nationwide.[52]

Those involved in birth centers are advocates of low-cost, consumer controlled, comprehensive maternity care. Birth centers are generally licensed by the state health division in which they are located. They are staffed by certified nurse-midwives, consulting physicians, registered nurses and dieticians, and other ancillary medical professionals. The centers provide pregnant women and their families with regular prenatal examinations and educational classes in family health and nutrition, physical fitness, childbirth, and parenting. A support person selected by the pregnant woman, most often but not necessarily the father-to-be, is a critical member of the health care team and participates in all phases of the mother's care. Women are carefully screened for potential complications during pregnancy or delivery and only low-risk mothers who anticipate normal, natural childbirth are accepted. In the unlikely event that complications do arise, the childbearing woman and midwife are transferred to the local general hospital (which must be located less than ten minutes away by car or ambulance).

While the specialized spaces within the hospital obstetrical unit historically isolated the mother, father, and newborn, and separated birth into a series of discrete stages monitored by different medical personnel according to staff availability and doctors' schedules, birth centers are designed to foster consumer control and the experience of childbirth as a normal and joyous part of the human life-cycle. Architecturally, the birth center has no actual prototype; but in familiar terms it combines clinical (hospital), educational (school), and

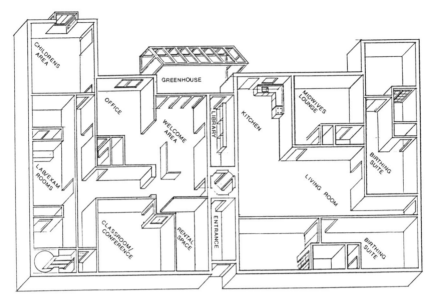

Figure 8. Axonometric drawing of a birth center designed by the architect to provide comprehensive prenatal care and family birthing suites with shared lounge and kitchen. Drawing courtesy Barbara Marks, architect.

residential (homelike) elements into two distinctly different spatial realms: prenatal and birthing (see fig. 8). The prenatal realm houses exam rooms, classrooms which double as exercise rooms, interview and conference spaces, reception and administration, reference/library space, rest rooms, and a child-minding or play space. Sometimes a "swap shop" for used baby clothing and furniture is included.

By the time of delivery, the center is already a familiar, friendly environment to the childbearing woman and her support person. Once they enter the birthing realm, they are made to feel at home; the midwife is considered their guest. Typically the birthing suite includes a bedroom, a family gathering room for waiting and celebrations, kitchen and eating facilities, and toilets with a large shower or bath. Sometimes the kitchen/eating and lounge area is shared among birthing couples who have their own private bedrooms for delivery and recovery. Midwives are provided with an enclosed rest area, a work space, storage, and laundry facilities. Couples are encouraged to personalize their birth environment by bringing their own sheets, pillows, food, music, and mementos.

The birthing realm is designed to allow the couple, with their family and friends, to progress comfortably together through the stages of labor. The parturient woman is free to walk around, join the others, eat something, shower, or retire to the bedroom and be alone. The nurse-midwife, already a close friend having provided months of prenatal care, is present to assist the couple during labor and delivery.

Following the birth, the new family remains in the birthing suite to celebrate, rest, and unite. Typically, they leave the birth center with their newborn within eight to twelve hours after delivery. Follow-up phone calls and home visits by the birth center staff during the early postpartum days, and return visits to the center for well-baby and well-woman care are common procedures.[53]

In the United States in 1989, the average cost of the comprehensive maternity care offered by birth centers was $2,111 compared to $3,960 for a private physician and a two-day hospital stay. The cost of anesthesia, ultrasound, fetal monitoring, or intravenous treatment is extra.[54] Nevertheless, since government Medicaid does not usually reimburse or reimburses only a small part of these costs, most low-income women cannot afford this less expensive, personalized care. However, since cost savings are often in excess of 50 percent compared to hospital care, private insurance companies such as Blue Cross and Blue Shield and Health Insurance Associations of America support birth centers. Certainly these reimbursements are essential if birth centers are to exist as a viable option.

To date, most birth centers have not been designed and built from scratch, but have entailed the adaptive reuse of an existing structure, from residential to office-type buildings. A small, human scale and an easily comprehensible spatial organization that offers flexibility and freedom of movement are important design considerations. Architectural details should reflect and support the values of those who use the center. Acoustical devices such as a heavy wood door on the birthing room, wall insulation, and the use of sound-absorbing materials like carpeting and drapery should be employed to allow a laboring woman to scream if she wants to without disturbing others. The entry to the birthing realm should be designed to mark the special, private event that will occur inside, in contrast to the publicly open entrance to the prenatal realm. Birthing rooms should be large enough to accommodate family members and to include double beds (for the couple to rest in). Showers and baths to relax in after the hard work of labor should be large enough to share with the father, the new infant, or a friend. Access to spaces that reinforce the continuity of nature's cycles of growth should be included: a quiet little garden, an atrium or greenhouse window, a reflection pool, wells of natural light, views of the sky or a tree that vividly displays the color of the season.

Although birth centers offer an exciting opportunity for innovative architectural expression, the opportunities to design and build them will be few if the wishes of the American medical profession prevail. Instead of seeing birth centers as an additive component to the maternity care network, they see them, and the midwives who run them, as competition that threatens their own medical monopoly over childbirth. Fearful of the declining birth rate and a dwindling patient load, since the early 1980s American doctors have been directing their lobbying efforts at the regional and state agencies responsible for approving new health care facilities like birth centers. As a result, the dominant trend in American obstetrics today is toward more centralized care. Small hospitals are closing their maternity wards in favor of large regional medical centers equipped with an even more elaborate range of staff and advanced equipment such as specialized neonatal units, which doctors believe all women should have available.[55] In some areas, the physicians are directing their efforts at preventing the practice of the nurse-midwives who are the primary care-givers at birth centers. Stories of harassment, discriminatory insurance policies, and midwife "burnout" are commonplace.[56]

Then, too, most states have not developed the licensing requirements and construction codes necessary to build birth centers. Currently, the centers fall between the code categories that apply to institutional facilities and those for business occupancy. These codes determine, for example, the type of fire protection, security, sanitation, use, and occupancy legally allowed for different types of buildings in order to protect the safety of those who will use them. Codes also indirectly determine the construction costs and operational overhead. An institutional facility must meet the strict requirements for an overnight stay; a business occupancy need not, and therefore costs less to build and operate, with the savings ultimately passed along to the consumer. Initiatives from architects and midwives are needed to help develop appropriate standards for birth centers.

Despite these obstacles, Kitty Ernst, director of the National Association of Childbearing Centers, anticipates a substantial growth in the number of birth centers throughout the 1990s. (She thinks the same is true for other ambulatory facilities like surgical centers and emergency care centers.) The reason? "High-tech machinery in hospitals is grinding up the health care dollars. Insurance carriers and consumers simply can't afford to ignore the fact that for almost twenty years birth centers have consistently demonstrated that they can deliver high quality, comprehensive maternity care at half the cost of an acute care facility," says Ernst.[57]

There is a third birth environment option, the mother's home. Statistics show that home births are safer than hospital births as long as a normal delivery is anticipated and especially if the birth is supervised by a trained midwife or obstetrician.[58] Advocates also claim that the social and emotional family-centered values of home birth far outweigh the risk there is for the family who chooses it.

Of all the options available, successful home birth is the most threatening to the medical establishment. About 5 percent of women attempting birth at home need to be transported to hospitals in spite of careful screening to ensure that they are at low risk.[59] When the laboring women arrive, some hospitals refuse to admit them; others have their babies taken away for a week or more as a form of punishment under the guise of monitoring the baby because it was placed at higher risk through lack of proper medical attention. One midwife commented: "A home birth person going to a hospital is like a woman with a misperformed abortion going to a Catholic hospital."[60] Also, most major insurance companies, in economic partnership with physicians, refuse to reimburse for home births.

Although the natural childbirth movement and the women's movement have together improved the chances for a better experience in childbirth, they have not altered birth in America in any fundamental way. Even though many women know that 95 percent of births are "normal" and "safe," the majority prefer to trust doctors, drugs, and traditional hospitals to produce "healthful births" instead of depending upon themselves, their own natural processes, midwives, birth centers, or home births. In 1989, 99 percent of American babies were born in hospitals.[61] However, hospitals have been forced to change their conventional policies and practices. Today most older hospitals have converted their labor rooms into small "LDR units," where labor, delivery, and recovery all take place. The mother is almost never moved except to postpartum, and friends and family can be present at most times. In newer hospitals, birthing rooms are being built to delivery-room codes by including medical gases, equipment, and mechanical systems cleverly hidden behind wall panels and cabinets, ensuring the doctor's comfort and convenience while maintaining the homelike atmosphere preferred by consumers.[62]

Of course, the general cultural preference for hospital births has been carefully and skillfully manufactured by the medical profession to ensure that the drama of birth takes place in the hospital's "operating theater" with the physician in the leading role. While the medical benefits of advanced obstetrical technologies and surgical techniques offered by hospitals can be of incomparable, life-saving importance to those who need them, most women do not. Insurance companies know this. Many carriers currently project that in the future, all normal vaginal deliveries will be on an out-patient basis.[63]

Whether a woman gives birth at home, in a birth center, a hospital birthing room, or the hospital's labor/delivery unit, the choice should be hers. The question of birth is really a question of woman's power or powerlessness. Man has exploited woman's childbearing like a crude, natural resource needing to be "processed" and "refined" in the factorylike assembly line of the hospital's obstetrical ward. To change this historically male-controlled experience of childbirth is to change women's relationship to powerlessness and fear, to their bodies, to their children, and to men.

The Spatial Pattern of Social Integration

The architecture of corporate towers, department stores, and shopping malls designed in relationship to economic production and consumption, and maternity hospitals designed in relationship to the economic and political control of human reproduction, rationalizes and institutionalizes prevailing notions of social caste. Any miscarriage of the spatial enactment of these caste distinctions is perceived by those who support the social order as profoundly threatening to the "stability" of society. For example, the contemporary movement to ensure women choices in childbearing and reproductive rights is characterized by impassioned controversy and even violence; for home birth implies that the doctor's specialized tools and skill are unnecessary; birth centers provide certified nurse-midwives with an autonomous workplace in which to demonstrate professional competence; and abortion clinics offer women legal, nonjudgmental, medically safe environments in which to decide for themselves whether or not to bring a pregnancy to term. Each alternative architectural setting seriously threatens the male establishment's monopoly over childbearing.

Similarly, the racial integration of public spaces and buildings was historically met with violence, angry resistance, and often utterly irrational reactions among those defending the status quo. In one instance, when automobiles were first made available to the public in the early 1900s, a white man in Macon County, Georgia, proposed that either "cars be taken away from Negroes or that the county maintain two separate systems of roads, one for whites and one for

Negroes."[64] Clearly, cars on the highways could not be segregated as easily as black and white passengers on trains or buses.

Many of the most courageous early opponents of such obdurate racial segregation were black women like the distinguished attorney Pauli Murray, who, as a law student at Howard University in the late 1930s, led a sit-in by black students at the public cafeteria in the United States Congress building to protest segregation;[65] or Mary Church Terrell, educator, suffragist, and political organizer, whose successful lawsuit against a Washington, D.C., restaurant that refused to serve her in 1950 judicially ended segregation in that city;[66] or Rosa Parks, a black seamstress in Alabama whose refusal, in 1956, to move to the back of a bus sparked the Montgomery bus boycott.[67] Like their sisters in the civil rights movement, feminists active in the women's movement throughout the nineteenth and twentieth centuries have worked indefatigably at the politics of integration— demanding that the doors of universities, corporate boardrooms, and factories be equally open to women as well as men, to racial and ethnic minorities as well as to the white majority.

However, although these efforts are necessary and worthy, the ultimate goal of feminism must not be the integration of women and minorities into "mainstream" society, but rather the abolition of patriarchy itself. By its very definition, a patriarchal society depends upon the unequal distribution of social resources and social power among many fragmented groups. Patriarchy pits one oppressed group against another in a hierarchy of oppression. Patriarchal thinking would have us separate and assign greater meaning to the suffering of a raped white woman or a lynched black man. In such a society, no one has a monopoly on oppression, and "equality" is an illusion. Any feminist analysis of gender oppression that fails to address simultaneously race and class is simpleminded and inadequate. Patriarchy constructs an architecture of exclusion that segregates and manipulates people according to social caste. Feminism would have us build an architecture of inclusion designed to provide all who use it with control and choice—from comprehending how to enter and leave a building, to being able to turn the lights on and off, adjust the heat, open a window, and lock a door. Large-scale public buildings like office towers and hospitals need not be intimidating, impersonal, and confusing; and congenial places of public assembly can be created in settings other than shopping malls designed solely to support the activities of conspicuous consumption. We must, however, recognize that the spatial form of public architecture is but a reflection of a comprehensive system of institutionalized racism, sexism, and classism that must first be understood and then transformed in order to change realistically the "institutional" buildings it produces.

NOTES

1. Sylvia Rodgers, "Women's Space in a Man's House: The British House of Commons," in *Women and Space*, ed. Ardener, 53.

2. Lisa Belkin, "Seeking Some Relief, She Stepped Out of Line," *New York Times*, 21 July 1990, 6.

3. Ibid.

4. Ibid.

5. Ibid. For a humorous discussion of public restroom facilities for women, see Margery Eliscu, "Bathrooms by the Marquis de Sade," in *In Stitches: A Patchwork of Feminist Humor and Satire*, ed. Gloria Kaufman (Bloomington: Indiana University Press, 1991), 110-12.

6. "Woman Is Acquitted in Trial for Using the Men's Room," *New York Times*, 3 November 1990, 8L.

7. Belkin, "Seeking Some Relief," 6.

8. Ibid., and "Woman Is Acquitted," 8L.

9. "Woman Is Acquitted," 8L.

10. Ibid.

11. Louis H. Sullivan, "The Tall Office Building Artistically Considered," *Kindergarten Chats* (New York: George Wittenborn, 1947, originally pub. 1896), 203.

12. Nancy Henley, *Body Politics* (Englewood Cliffs, N.J.: Prentice Hall, 1977), 36.

13. Hayden, "Skyscraper Seduction," 112.

14. Mary Kathleen Benet, *The Secretarial Ghetto* (New York: McGraw-Hill, 1972), as quoted in Madonna Kolbenschlage, *Kiss Sleeping Beauty Good-Bye* (New York: Bantam Books, 1981), 86.

15. Jonathan Goldman and Michael Valenti, *The Empire State Building Book* (New York: St. Martin's, 1980), 30.

16. Ibid., 92–93.

17. Hayden, "Skyscraper Seduction," 109.

18. Elizabeth Lindquist-Cock and Estelle Jussim, "Machismo in American Architecture," *The Feminist Art Journal* (Spring 1974):9–10.

19. Ibid.

20. Altman and Chemers, *Culture and Environment*, 299–300.

21. Paolo Soleri, *Arcology: The City in the Image of Man* (Cambridge, Mass.: MIT Press, 1969).

22. The term "architectural machismo" is taken from Lindquist-Cock and Jussim, "Machismo in American Architecture," 9–10.

23. Ibid., 9–10, and Hayden, "Skyscraper Seduction," 112–13.

24. Philip Johnson is the architect of the controversial 645-foot-high $200

million AT&T World Headquarters in New York City, whose pedimented top has caused it to be likened to a piece of Chippendale furniture. Johnson, in partnership with Texan developer Gerald Hines, has built eleven high rises across America, and in December 1983 he unveiled his model for the first oval skyscraper to be built in New York City. Jane Ellis, "Trends," *New York Post*, 19 December 1983, 19.

25. Susan Porter Benson, "Palace of Consumption and Machine for Selling: The American Department Store, 1880–1940," *Radical History Review* 21 (Fall 1979): 202. Also see idem, *Counter Cultures* (Urbana: University of Illinois Press, 1986).

26. Sheila Rothman, *Woman's Proper Place* (New York: Basic Books, 1978), 19–20.

27. Ibid., 21.

28. Benson, "Palace of Consumption," 205.

29. Ibid., 207.

30. Ibid., 208.

31. Ibid.

32. For a well-illustrated book on international shopping mall design see Barry Maitland, *Shopping Malls, Planning and Design* (New York: Nichols, 1985).

33. William Severini Kowinski, *The Malling of America* (New York: William Morrow, 1985), 22.

34. Ann Tooley, "The Mall: A Woman's World," *US News and World Report*, 31 July 1989, 66.

35. Kowinski, *Malling of America*, 182.

36. Maitland, *Shopping Malls*, 67–68, 82–90.

37. Richard W. Wertz and Dorothy C. Wertz, *Lying In: A History of Childbirth in America* (New York: Schocken, 1977), 80–84; and David Rosner, "Social Control and Social Service: The Changing Use of Space in Charity Hospitals," *Radical History Review 21*, "The Spatial Dimensions of History" (Fall 1979): 183–85.

38. Wertz and Wertz, *Lying In*, 47, 54, 143, 145.

39. Adrienne Rich, *Of Woman Born* (New York: W. W. Norton, 1976), 144, 146, 147.

40. Wertz and Wertz, *Lying In*, 161, 163.

41. Ibid., 154, 155.

42. Ibid., 156, 157.

43. Ibid., 158, 159.

44. Ibid., 159, 167.

45. Suzanne Arms, *Immaculate Deception* (Boston: Houghton Mifflin, 1975), 186.

46. Wertz and Wertz, *Lying In*, 170.

47. Ibid., 197.

48. Ibid., 171.

49. Ibid.

50. Ibid., 172.

51. Ibid., 195.

52. "Choices in Childbirth," *New Woman's Times* (June 1984):4; and Kitty Ernst, Director, National Association of Childbearing Centers, Perkiomenville, Pennsylvania, interview with Leslie Kanes Weisman, 21 August 1989.

53. Leslie Kanes Weisman with Susana Torre, "Restoring Women's Birth-Rights," *The Matriarchist* 1, no. 4 (1977): 4; and Susana Torre and Leslie Kanes Weisman, "Birth Center Design Studio Program" and Exhibition at New Jersey Institute of Technology, School of Architecture, Newark, 1977.

54. Ernst, interview.

55. Wertz and Wertz, *Lying In*, 241.

56. "Choices in Childbirth," 5–6.

57. Ernst, interview.

58. Wertz and Wertz, *Lying In*, 239–41.

59. Ibid., 241.

60. "Choices in Childbirth," 7.

61. Ernst, interview.

62. Jan Bishop, principal and director of Health Care Architecture, Ewing, Cole, Cherry, and Parsky, Philadelphia, Pennsylvania, interview with Leslie Kanes Weisman, 18 May 1991.

63. Ibid.

64. Joseph Interrante, "You Can't Go to Town in a Bathtub: Automobile Movement and the Reorganization of Rural American Space, 1900–1930," *Radical History Review* 21 (Fall 1979): 161.

65. Casey Miller and Kate Swift, "Pauli Murray," *Ms.*, March 1980, 64.

66. Bettina Aptheker, *Women's Legacy: Essays on Race, Sex, and Class in American History* (Amherst: University of Massachusetts Press, 1982), 149.

67. Ibid., 149–50.

3

The Private Use of
Public Space

Like the public buildings discussed in the previous chapter, the contemporary urban landscape is a paradigmatic stage set for the workings of patriarchy. In city streets, parks, and neighborhoods, territorial dramas between women and men, rich and poor are enacted daily. Each group "appears" in public and claims and uses public space according to its socially prescribed roles. Those with power, for example "street gangs," control the streets and the people on them. Those without power, like the "street dweller" and the "street walker," are relegated to the streets where their private lives are on public display. Though they are all "at home" on the streets, "home" means something very different to each.

People also consider themselves "at home" in certain neighborhoods, and refer to cities as "hometowns" and to nations as "homelands." As with the streetscape, how people experience and inhabit these "public homes," what these places mean, physically and symbolically, depends upon their "social place" and the extent to which they accept or challenge it.

City Streets and Sexual Geography

Armed with a piece of chalk, children can turn public sidewalks into private gameboards that block pedestrian traffic. Armed with a can of spray paint, teenagers can turn the walls of public buildings and highway overpasses into private billboards. Armed with society's tacit approval, men can turn allegedly public city streets into a private male jungle where women are excluded or, in the words of the poet Marge Piercy, "stalked like the tame pheasants who are hand-raised and then turned loose for hunters to shoot, an activity called sport."[1]

Male street gangs, and a high incidence of related vandalism and crime, are familiar facts of urban life. So are the "gang wars" that erupt when one group invades the neighborhood "turf" of another. The widespread availability of crack cocaine is accelerating murders among members of rival gangs competing to get rich selling the savage drug. In such encounters, in the slums' streets, and in the company of male peers, the ghetto boy is socialized to his male role.

Boys "grow up" in the streets where they learn the lessons of manhood. "Nice girls" are kept off the streets and close to home, lest their virginity or virtue or both be endangered. Most men are "at home" on the streets; most women are not. "I always thought of Harlem as home," wrote Claude Brown, "but I never thought of Harlem as being in the house. To me, home was the streets."[2]

It is no coincidence that every city has a "porno strip." Along these streetscapes of depravity, misogynistic messages packaged as pleasure, seduction, and erotica bombard the senses: in the ghostly neon signs of tawdry bars featuring topless "Go-go Girls" dancing in cages; in the flashing marquees of "live peep shows" and "adult" movie houses showing women being cut into parts with a chain saw or tied up, raped, and sodomized with a rifle by an ex-Marine who misses combat; in the porn book stores selling magazines like *Bondage* or *Hustler* where "Chester the Molester" molests a different young girl each month using techniques like lying, kidnaping, and assault.[3]

But the porno strip is not the only public place where crude and dehumanizing sex-role stereotypes appear. The entire urban environment is filled with images of macho men and sexually submissive women. Commercial billboards depicting rugged cowboys smoking cigarettes appear in marked contrast to the smiling seduction of scantily clad models selling designer jeans and expensive liquor. Compare, too, the bronze statues of male war heroes and politicians in whose honor our public parks are named, with the nude vulnerability of the female nymphs and goddesses that decorate the fountains of those same public parks, and the pairs of bare-breasted caryatids who, in eternal servitude, support with their heads the weight of building entablatures over the entrances of neoclassical apartments and office buildings.

The exploitive double standard between the sexes that the public landscape communicates so vividly is regularly enacted on the public streets themselves, in the "respectable" male pastime known as "girl watching." Few women, whether they like it or not, escape the silent eyes, "friendly" comments, blown kisses, clucks, whistles, and obscene gestures men presume they can impose upon any woman passing by.

Such invasive male behavior violates a woman's self/other boundary, leaving her enraged, startled, humiliated, and unable to control her own privacy. Even those women who have learned to "handle" these situations with skilled retort cannot escape the overriding message of male power. This double standard has contributed to what John Berger calls a "split consciousness" in public space. In his book *Ways of Seeing,* Berger explains: "Men act, and women appear. Men look at women. Women watch themselves being looked at."[4]

Women, thus unable to regulate their interactions with male strangers in public places, are robbed of an important privilege of urban life: their anonymity. Women learn to be constantly on the alert, both consciously and unconsciously, in order to protect vulnerable boundaries from male trespasses. Researchers have demonstrated that women avoid eye contact, stiffen body posture, restrict movements, and move out of the way of pedestrian traffic more than men, a pattern of submissive behavior observed in animal societies.[5] Irwin Altman, a psychologist, maintains that this behavior requires an enormous amount of energy which "places great stress on adrenal and cardiovascular systems, resulting in heightened psychological tension and anxiety . . . [and] psychic damage."[6]

If the fear of sexual harassment on the street causes women stress, the fear of rape keeps women off the streets at night, away from public parks and "dangerous" parts of town, and unconsciously afraid of half the human race. Women learn that any man is a potential abuser and any place where men are found can threaten their safety. Contrary to popular belief, men do not rape because they are out of control but as a way of maintaining it. Rape is the most paradigmatic means of social control. Its unmistakable intention is to keep all women in "their place," in "line," and in a constant state of fear.

Eventually women come to understand that the public streets and parks belong to men. Further, women are constantly reminded by rapists, police officers, and judges of their responsibility to uphold this social norm and the dangerous consequences of their failure to do so. Statements like this one made by a police superintendent are not infrequent: "Any woman walking alone after dark invites trouble."[7] Neither are court decisions that blame the victim unusual. For example, in England in 1982 a judge ruled that a man who pleaded guilty to raping a seventeen-year-old woman should be fined the equivalent of four hundred dollars instead of receiving a jail sentence because the rape victim was "guilty of a great deal of contributory negligence"—she had been hitchhiking late at night.[8] In 1986, a Washington judge sentences a rape victim to thirty days in jail for being in contempt of court; terrified of seeing the rapist again, she had refused to testify against him. The chief prosecutor said, "I hate to see the victim treated worse than the defendant, but I don't see any other alternative."[9] Today, news reports of rapes and incidents of "wilding" (in which gangs of very young boys "entertain" themselves by premeditated violent assault) have become a "normal" part of daily television and radio.

It stands to reason that if women perceive public space as unmanageable and threatening, they will avoid it and restrict their mobility within it. This phenomenon, according to a study by Elizabeth W. Markson and Beth B. Hess, exists most dramatically among urban, elderly women, particularly those with limited educations who live alone in apartments. Many of these women are afraid to leave their homes. They are especially frightened of going out at night and curtail their social lives accordingly.[10]

Markson and Hess believe the mass media foster the notion of the powerlessness of older women, particularly poor and minority women, and grossly exaggerate the amount of crime perpetrated against them. They refer to a survey of violence depicted on TV shows in which the most frequent victims were children, old women, nonwhite women, and lower-class women. While they found that TV killers were most often men, murder victims were most frequently old, poor, urban women. Further, in TV news broadcasts, the most publicized cases of violence, despite the fact that these were not the most common cases, involved black assailants and white victims.[11] It offends that any woman or man should be attacked; but it is equally offensive that so many women live in fear of attack, and that those fears are manipulated to perpetuate racism and effectively imprison women in their own homes.

Withdrawal in response to the dangers of urban life leaves the streets open to criminal behavior. Eventually business conditions deteriorate, the quality of life of the entire community is eroded, and neighborhood collapse is inevitable. If the demise of our inner cities is to be reversed, women's fear and victimization must be reduced. To do so, politicians and municipal service agencies must admit that violence against women and children is pervasive; that women's fears are based in reality; and that women know when they feel unsafe in cities, and why.

Toronto's METRAC project provides an excellent model. The Metro Action Committee on Public Violence Against Women and Children (METRAC) was established in 1984 by the council of metropolitan Toronto. It succeeds a task force initiated by the council in 1982 to address the concerns of women in Toronto after a series of rape-murders in the city. The eighty volunteer members of the task force—doctors, lawyers, politicians, police, social workers, urban planners, workers from rape crisis centers, and other women's organizations—developed a comprehensive, multidisciplinary approach to violence protection that METRAC has carried forward in its work to make the city safe for women and children.

The METRAC staff (all women) stresses the importance of consulting with women in any project they undertake. A number of their initiatives concentrate on urban and architectural design, since various physical/geographical features may enhance or detract from the use of a particular site for assault. METRAC is responsible for the review and improvement of standards of lighting, signage, and security in all underground parking garages in Toronto; has conducted safety audits of the city's subway system and bus routes in collaboration with the police force and the Toronto Transit Commission; and has worked with the Parks and Recreation Department on a safety audit directed toward sexual assault prevention in High Park (the city's largest park). In the latter instance, METRAC observed that in the 1987 user study on park safety initiated by the department, vandalism and boating safety were addressed but women's concerns were ignored. METRAC intervened and invited women from Women Plan Toronto, the High Park Women's Action Committee, and other women park users to join in day and night-time "walkabouts" to assess existing conditions and suggest changes that would make the park feel and be safer. The factors they considered included: lighting, sightlines/visibility, entrapment possibilities, ear and eye distance, movement predictors (such as pathways and tunnels), signage/information, visibility of park staff/police, public telephones, assailant escape routes, maintenance levels (for example, neglected areas or replacing damaged lights and signs), parks programming information, and isolation (one of the biggest factors in feeling safe or unsafe). With this input, METRAC prepared a report, *Planning for Sexual Assault Prevention: Women's Safety in High Park* (January 1989), that included fifty-five recommendations to the Parks and Recreation Department. For example, emergency telephones, maps showing park layout, and signs along the trails indicating that a user is only a two-minute walk from the restaurant or swimming pool would help counter feelings of isolation and suggest where help could be found if needed without destroying the enjoyable feeling of seclusion in the park.

METRAC has also produced the groundbreaking *WISE (Women in Safe Environments) Report* documenting the design characteristics that contribute to women's feeling unsafe in public places (poor lighting, being deserted, not being visible to others, and having no access to help are qualities that are high on the list) and a Safety Audit Kit that women can use to evaluate dangerous areas of the city, their home neighborhoods, and their workplaces. In 1990 METRAC began the preparation of a discussion paper on women's safety and urban/architectural design in order to facilitate the development of criteria for guidelines and standards for all buildings in the city—construction and renovation projects, shopping centers, housing projects, parks, and all other public spaces.[12]

Assaults in urban public places, to a great degree, are crimes of opportunity. While the design of our physical surroundings does not cause sexual assault, it plays a significant part in creating opportunities for it. Those who are vulnerable—women, children, the disabled, and elderly people—have the right to safe access to the cities in which they live. Preventing sexual assault against women by deliberate planning and assessment results in urban and architectural design that enhances everyone's safety.

The Street as Extension of the Domestic Environment

While countless women are trapped in their own homes by fear of the streets, one of the ironies of contemporary society is that countless others are forced to make their living on the streets. Because there are so few safe shelters for prostitutes, there is little opportunity for them to escape from street violence and dependence on abusive pimps. Indeed, prostitutes report that sex itself has become more violent. In 1986 an average of one prostitute a month was murdered in Los Angeles, according to a police report.[13] Often the experience of violence in the home—from incest and sexual abuse to battering— drives women into prostitution. They are runaways and pushed-aways who continue as prostitutes because of economic necessity. The "streetwalker's" appearance in public implies that she belongs to no man and therefore belongs to all men. She is a surrogate wife practicing the sexual rituals enacted in the private family home on the anonymous public streets of patriarchy.

In a different way, the street is literally home to tens of thousands of homeless people. In 1989, American estimates ranged from the government claim of 350,000 to the Coalition for the Homeless estimate of 3 million homeless nationwide; and if current federal policies continue, there will be 18 million homeless people by the year 2000.[14] They are found in every city, lying on sidewalks and in the doorways of shabby hotels and cheap bars, sleeping in abandoned buildings, over hot-air grates, in trash dumpsters, phone booths, train stations, and airports. The lucky find refuge in shelters and missions dispensing salvation and a free meal.

In the 1960s the homeless were mostly all older, white, male alcoholics or drifters who lived on "skid row." In the 1980s they were increasingly women, blacks, families, people with AIDS (PWA's), and younger men averaging in their low thirties in age. Most of the men were the local unemployed or unemployable who left high schools and housing projects without job skills.[15]

Homeless PWA's are a relatively heterogeneous group. They are mainly minorities who became HIV infected through intravenous drug use by themselves or their sexual partners. They are single men and women, families, single parents, abandoned children, and teenagers whose infection is concomitant to their life on the streets.

If these people are not already homeless, their illness often precipitates their homelessness. Unable to work, they cannot pay rent. Others are illegally evicted by AIDS-phobic landlords. Compared to the need, the amount of housing assistance currently available for homeless PWA's is insignificant. For example, in 1989 in New York City, fewer than eighty apartments were available specifically for homeless people with AIDS; yet the Partnership for the Homeless estimated that there were five thousand to eight thousand homeless New Yorkers with AIDS and related HIV illness that year. By 1993 they say the figure will jump to thirty thousand, making PWA's the largest subgroup among New York City's homeless.[16]

During the 1980s, the number of homeless single women increased by an average of 16 percent in twenty-one of twenty-six cities surveyed by the US Conference of Mayors.[17] In 1989, single women and their children constituted a staggering 86 percent of homeless families in New York, according to a study done by the city's Human Resources Administration.[18]

Single women and women heading families are burgeoning among the homeless as a result of government cuts in disability benefits, rising housing costs, an increase in divorce rates, domestic violence, teenage pregnancies, and increasing poverty caused by unemployment, low-paying jobs, and wage discrimination. In 1980, two out of every three adults with incomes below the poverty level were women, and over half of all poor families were female headed.[19]

Homeless single women and women with children have been joined by huge numbers of predominantly female mental patients released by unspeakably overcrowded and inhumane state mental

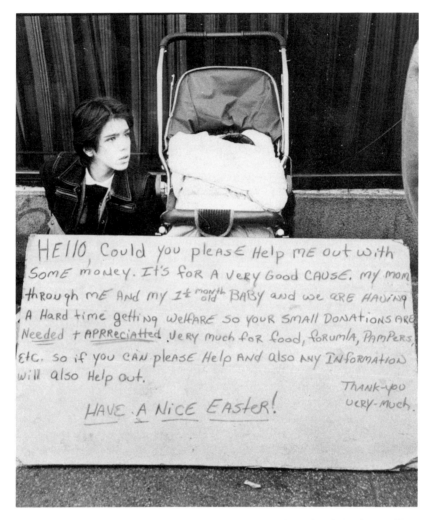

Figure 9. A young teen mother and her infant are forced to join the swelling ranks of homeless women and children in New York City. Photograph courtesy Bettye Lane.

institutions responding to pressures to deinstitutionalize the nondangerous mentally ill. Between 1955 and 1982 the population in state mental institutions in America shrank by more than three-quarters.[20] But programs for "independent living" in local community facilities were never adequately funded, leaving countless thousands of patients homeless and on their own.

In addition, America's failed housing policies have swollen the ranks of the homeless. Since the 1960s, Washington has wasted billions of dollars on administratively inept public housing programs that ended up subsidizing middle-class renters instead of the poor—composed predominantly of women and children—and has built less than half of the six million low-income housing units President Lyndon Johnson believed were needed in 1968. Between 1978 and 1988, appropriations for federal subsidized housing programs declined by more than 80 percent, from $32.2 billion to $9.8 billion.[21] Under the Reagan administration new construction dwindled to 55,120 units in 1983, despite the mind-numbing waiting periods for public housing: four years in Savannah, Georgia, twelve in New York, and twenty in Miami.[22] Instead, President Reagan opted to base his housing policy on $200 million in rent vouchers for low-income people—a plan that mistakenly assumed there was no housing shortage, only a shortage of money to pay for it. (In 1984, the Brookings Institution estimated that in 1990 the shortage of low-income units could reach 1.7 million.)[23]

In a break with the Reagan administration, President George Bush's budget for fiscal year 1990 included $1.1 billion to fund fully the Stewart B. McKinney Homeless Assistance Act. However, while it is encouraging that more money will be spent on emergency aid, the Bush budget contains no provision to increase low-income housing. Rather, it retains the Reagan administration's 18.6 percent cut in housing programs by $1.7 billion, despite the fact that in 1989, among the estimated twenty-nine million Americans who needed low-income housing, only one in four had access to it.[24]

A substantial percentage of America's homeless are victims of "urban revitalization." As cities began to rejuvenate their deteriorating downtowns in the 1970s, the sleazy welfare hotels and flophouses, called "SRO's" for "single-room occupancies," were among the first buildings to be torn down or converted to condominiums for the affluent. SRO's provide furnished rooms with shared bathrooms and communal kitchens and dining facilities. The presence of a manager or clerk "at the desk" twenty-four hours a day can also provide immediate assistance to residents and a sense of security, especially for older women who are often afraid of their living environment.

Conditions in SRO's vary from comfortable to deplorable. None of the residents is eligible for shelter assistance as government regulations require recipients to live in a "self-contained" dwelling unit (one that includes a private toilet and kitchen). But the furnished room with available services such as meals, linen, and housekeeping is a viable housing choice for many older people who do not need institutional care. Nonetheless, the number of SRO's was reduced by nearly one-half the national total between 1970 and 1980, a loss of about one million rooms.[25]

Instead of destroying this housing we should be upgrading substandard conditions through code enforcement, authorizing government supplements to the occupants, and working to improve the social environment for the older, noncriminal population that is forced to live side-by-side with addicts and alcoholics. Urban renewal and city programs that eliminate or close SRO's displace thousands of the very poorest and frailest, a dramatic proportion consisting of minority and white, ethnic, elderly people and single mothers who are literally dumped into the streets, often with little or no warning and with no affordable place to go.

Confronted with nowhere to live, the homeless must then face the paradox of their own "ineligibility" for social support service. Without a home address they do not qualify, in most states, for foodstamps or welfare. Without a mailing address, they are unable to obtain copies of legal documents, such as birth certificates, required for public assistance. The result is an entire underclass of people who have slipped through the "safety nets" and into the gutter.[26]

Life on the street is a world filled with hunger, illness, hallucinations, and exposure to suffocating heat, freezing cold, and constant danger. Street women, because they are women, are especially fearful of assault and rape. "Even the most deranged bag ladies [so named because they carry all their possessions with them in bags], who just want to be left alone, are vulnerable because of rumors that they keep money in their bags," wrote the journalist Patricia King in an article on Chicago's "street girls." One woman she interviewed told her, "On the streets . . . you have to have eyes behind your head and look like you're not scared."[27] Faced with the constant threat of violence, street women develop formidable defense strategies. They know that few people will bother them if they are filthy or appear to be insane.

A New York City "street girl" named Lea told Alan M. Beck and Philip Marden that she occasionally slept with other women in doorways for protection.[28] Beck and Marden also reported in their 1977 study, "Three women spent nearly all their time within a few blocks of each other. . . . Two of them told us that they chose the area because they thought it was safe. In other parts of the city, they were harassed by storekeepers or assaulted by hoodlums."[29]

Homeless women are not necessarily safer in the shelters. A report entitled "Victims Again" includes vivid testimony by eighty women living in two New York women's shelters of the myriad ways they are harassed by the shelter system itself—from physical abuse by crack-smoking guards to forced separation from friends, children, and other family members and the withholding of subway tokens for transportation. Women who live in shelters are frequently pressured to do staff jobs like cleaning hallways for ridiculous pay (usually sixty-three cents an hour). Meals are not kept available for those who work at real jobs outside the shelter; if the woman works a night shift she is still expected to leave the building by 8:00 A.M.; and pregnant women are generally not given prenatal care or additional food, or allowed extra bedrest.[30]

The homeless, women or men, live hard and certainly "deviant" lives. They have few resources available to them, but women seem to have the fewest. For example, in the city-run shelters for women and men in the area of New York City that Beck and Marden studied in 1977, the women's shelter had forty-seven beds and had to turn away two thousand women. (There were an estimated three thousand homeless women citywide that year.) At the same time, the men's shelter had room for several hundred and placed hundreds more in flophouse hotels where there were free meals and beds available for thousands of men. "They [men] are almost never denied a bed," wrote a shelter staff member.[31]

While the tragic plight of America's burgeoning homeless has become increasingly visible, there still seems to be a "visibility gap" between the sexes. For instance, in 1981 the following notice appeared in a New York state legislative report: "The 36,000 homeless people of New York City have won an important victory. . . . The city was forced to sign a consent decree in State Supreme Court mandating that shelter be provided to any man who seeks it this winter. While not specifically included in the decree, women will also benefit from the decision."[32] The notice did not go on to explain how.

To date, both public and private efforts to provide safe emergency housing for homeless women, men, and families have been sorely inadequate. In 1984 New York's public shelter system—the largest in the country—housed six thousand people in a city where there were an estimated twenty thousand homeless in the under-twenty-one age category alone.[33] All across the nation, shelters are too few and too lacking in beds, toilets, showers, privacy, sanitation, heat, and security. It is not uncommon to find fire escapes sealed shut, broken windows, clogged toilets, sporadic hot water, and infestations of rats and other rodents. This journalist's description of the Fort Washington Armory Men's Shelter in New York City is revealing:

More than 900 men sometimes sleep in rows of beds on a gymnasium floor the size of a football field. Although guards patrol here, as they do at all the shelters, new arrivals are warned to sleep with their shoes under the legs of their beds as protection against theft. The men have arranged the rows to form the remnants of boundaries they once called home—Spanish Harlem at one end, Harlem at the other, the Bronx and Brooklyn in the middle. In addition, the homeless men who earn $12.50 for 20 hours of menial work at the shelters sleep in a row along one wall that is known as Park Avenue.[34]

Among the homeless it is hard to tell those who were emotionally disturbed before they became homeless from those who were driven over the edge by the harshness of street life. Sometimes at shelters the seriously psychotic, alcoholics, and drug addicts wander freely among the simply down-and-out and can be very disruptive. Consequently, most shelters have regulations designed to restrict the behavior of all based on the behavior of few. Alcohol is usually banned from the premises; cigarette smoking is allowed only in certain areas; bathroom doors cannot be locked. Meals are usually provided by volunteers; cooking or self-service by residents is seldom allowed. Furnishings are often shabby, and sleeping arrangements are dormitorylike with little or no privacy. Few visitors are permitted, and when they are there is no place to entertain them, be they a relative, friend, or lover. This suggests that homeless people do not need privacy, self-expression, friendships, and sexual relations, or at least that these needs should not be taken seriously. Perhaps this explains why housing for the homeless is referred to as "shelter," meaning a roof over your head, rather than "home," which implies autonomy and emotional as well as material support. All things considered, it is understandable why many homeless people avoid shelters, preferring to take their chances on the street.

Of course, the enduring solution to homelessness is transitional housing that provides ongoing support such as job training, health care, and childcare, coupled with the availability of permanent low-cost housing. In the interim, emergency shelter must be small scale, humane, and free of the barbaric conditions that now characterize most of them.

Feminist Politics and Claiming Public Space

The lives of prostitutes and the homeless illustrate how city streets operate as theaters of social action in which women and others without social power are cast as marginalized "social deviants." The poli-

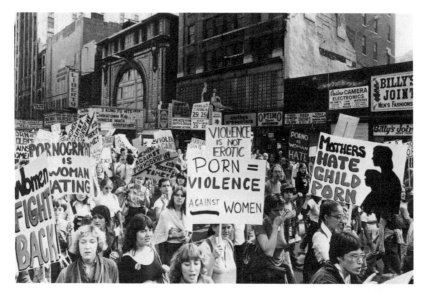

Figure 10. Women march on Forty-second Street, New York City's infamous porno strip, in an antipornography demonstration. Photograph courtesy Bettye Lane.

tics of public space belongs on the feminist agenda, for it is obvious that streets and parks, allegedly open to all people, are not open to all people equally. The denial of women's rights as citizens to equal access to public space—and of the psychological and physical freedom to use it in safety—has made public space, not infrequently, the testing ground of challenges to male authority and power. One of the most dramatic challenges occurred in San Francisco in 1978 when over five thousand women from thirty American states gathered at nightfall to march down the city's porno strip. Andrea Dworkin recalls: " . . . We wound our way toward Broadway, which was crowded with tourists, neon signs advertising live sex shows, adult bookstores, and pornographic theaters. Chanting slogans such as 'No More Profit off Women's Bodies,' we filled the streets entirely, blocking off traffic and completely occupying the Broadway strip for three blocks. For an hour, and for the first time ever, Broadway belonged not to the barkers, pimps, or pornographers, but instead to the songs, voices, rage and vision of thousands of women."[35] Similar marches have taken place in virtually every major city in the United States.

At a different but no less significant scale, small groups of women are using public space as an arena of personal protest. In October

1982 a dozen women at Brown University in Providence, Rhode Island, "equipped with bright red spray paint and stencils . . . splashed their message on university buildings, sidewalks, and stairwells: 'One in Three Women are Raped: Fight Back!' " The actions of the "graffitists," who call themselves Feminists Involved in Reaching Equality (FIRE), sparked a campus-wide controversy that produced a new women's peer counseling program, a night-time escort service run exclusively by women, and free courses in self-defense. As part of their efforts to raise consciousness, the FIRE women also posted official-looking curfew signs all over Providence mandating that men get off the streets in the evening, a suggestion first made by Israel's Prime Minister Golda Meir, who reasoned that if Israeli women were in danger of attack, a curfew should be placed on those causing the danger (men) and not, as her male colleagues suggested, on the victims.[36]

Women, too, are increasingly recognizing the connections between male violence in their own lives and male militarism on an international scale. From the Women's Peace Camp at Greenham Common in England to the Women's Pentagon Action (WPA) in Washington, D.C., women are refusing to accept life on the precipice, where the male war machine has placed us all, themselves included. On 27 August 1981, a group of English and Welsh women and children marched 125 miles from Cardiff in Wales to the U.S. Air Force base at Greenham Common near Newbury in Berkshire, where 96 cruise nuclear missiles were due to be deployed. They pitched their tents and vowed to stay until the deployment plan was scrapped. That was the state of the first women's peace camp, which has since become a worldwide phenomenon. Other camps have been formed in Italy, West Berlin, Scotland, northern Germany, Norway, Sweden, and in scattered sites in the United States.[37]

Within months after the establishment of the Greenham Common Camp, on 15 and 16 November 1981, the Women's Pentagon Action organized a peace march in which an estimated 4,500 women from across the United States and abroad converged on the Pentagon to mourn and express outrage at the ongoing acceleration of nuclear armament and the global oppression of women and other peoples. As they marched, the women wove a continuous braid which encircled the entire building. They wove a web of colored yarn across the doorways. As police cut away the web, the women tenaciously rewove the severed strands. At the end of the day, sixty-five women were arrested and imprisoned for civil disobedience.[38]

On 18 July 1983, fifty women created a women's peace camp in New York City's Bryant Park, just one block from the Times Square district, notorious for its muggings, drug dealing, and "flesh trafficking." The women camped out in the park for two weeks. Although Bryant Park officially closes each evening at nine o'clock, the police did not evict them. Supporters brought them food and water. The campers conducted street performances and symbolic rituals, organized peace walks, and distributed leaflets to publicize the opening of the Women's Encampment for a Future of Peace and Justice.[39]

This latter women's peace camp borders the Seneca Army Depot in New York State, the storage site for the neutron bombs and the point from which the United States deployed its Pershing II nuclear missiles to Greenham Common, as part of a NATO "peacekeeping" force. Five hundred women opened the camp on 4 July 1983, America's Independence Day, and during the next month over 3,000 women demonstrated in protest of deployment. More than 250 scaled the depot fence in a mass civil disobedience. All were arrested.[40]

It would be easy to dismiss these examples of nonviolent civil disobedience, demonstrations, and symbolic rituals as well-intended but naive and ultimately ineffective strategies for social change. After all, pornography is still a flourishing business, every ten minutes a woman is raped in America, and the nuclear arms race continues to threaten us all with extinction. But is direct efficacy the only purpose for political activism? I think not. Those who participate in group demonstrations find their personal beliefs affirmed and clarified; they experience solidarity with others and a renewed sense of energy and strength to confront and challenge injustice in their own daily lives.

If we define society as a human community, then the transformation of individual attitudes and values represents meaningful social change. Each time a person refuses to laugh at a racist joke, buy a pornographic magazine, use gender-exclusive language, or vote for nuclear "defense," then "society" is not the same, for its prevailing standards have been rejected and those who enforce them have been made to think about alternatives. This personalization of society is a radical notion since we are taught to imagine society as an abstraction of laws and government processes that exist beyond the reach of "ordinary" people. This dichotomy in the way society is conceptualized or experienced is connected to gender socialization.

Women's and men's self/other boundaries are shaped very differently, and consequently so are their views about war and peace. Carol Gilligan has done research on psychological theory that explains how women's moral development is deeply embedded in an ethic of responsibility to others that "bends" the rules to preserve relationships, while men's moral development is linked to respecting individual rights and learning to "play the game fair and square" according to the rules. Thus, men would logically view war as a "necessary game of political strategy" and the assertion of a moral imperative; women would view war as the cause of painful human suffering and loss on both "sides" and the senseless expression of "failed relationships."[41]

Both Gilligan and Jean Baker Miller, a psychotherapist and author of *Toward a New Psychology of Women* (1976), believe that men's sense of self is tied to a separation from others and to a belief in the "efficacy of aggression," women's to a "recognition of the need for connection" and the maintenance of a web of affiliations.[42] Thus, while the male-defined "morality of rights and justice" is based on a belief in equality, defined as the same treatment for everyone predicated on the understanding of fairness and autonomy, women's "ethic of responsibility and care" is based on a belief in nonviolence and equity, which recognizes differing needs and protects people from being hurt, predicated on the understanding of nurturance and attachment.[43]

These different modes of moral development for women and men give rise to different ways of evaluating the consequences of choice between violence and nonviolence. An event that occurred on 21 August 1976, in the battle-scarred streets of Belfast, Northern Ireland, provides an example. On that day, ten thousand Catholic and Protestant women—setting aside the centuries-old hatreds that have separated Northern Ireland's feuding communities, and in defiance of terrorist death threats against their lives—gathered with their children on the spot where, ten days before, three children had been killed by Irish Republican Army gunmen fleeing British troops. This mass peace rally, which resulted in the formation of the Peace Women's Movement (the name was later changed to the People for Peace Movement so that men would not feel excluded), was spearheaded by Betty Williams, an angry thirty-two-year-old Roman Catholic housewife who had witnessed the children's deaths. Mrs. Williams later recalled her feelings and actions:

> Did you ever get sick inside, so sick that you didn't even know what was wrong with you? I couldn't cook a dinner. I couldn't think straight. I couldn't even cry, and as the night went on I got angrier and angrier. . . . I . . . took an air-mail writing pad and I went right up to the heart of provisional IRA territory in Andersontown and I didn't knock at the door very nicely, by the way, I didn't say, "Excuse me. Would you like to sign this? We all want peace." I was spitting angry, and I banged the woman's door and she came. I frightened the life out of her. I really did. When she came out, I said, "Do you want peace?" She said "Yes!"

"Yes, then sign that." It sort of started out like that and it went on . . .
further down the street. . . . All the women felt that way. . . . We had
3,000 or 6,000 signatures in three hours. We went back to my home.
They were in the lounge. They were in the living room. They were in
the kitchen. They were in the hall. They were lined up the stairs. They
were in the bathroom, the two bedrooms. There just wasn't enough
room to hold them all, and they were all just as angry as I was . . . that
we had let this go on for so long.[44]

Long before the guns came out, housing, the central demand of
the civil rights movement in Northern Ireland, was crucial for Catholic women whose families were crammed into miserable tenements
and regularly denied houses to maintain the voter domination of
Protestant Unionist households. The thought of moving from a slum
flat to a modern house gave Catholic mothers everything to live for
and something worth dying for on the streets, on behalf of their
children.[45]

When women take to the streets in angry protest, it is consistent
with their sense of moral responsibility to care for others, and that
responsibility can transcend the boundaries of male-defined cultural
taboos. For example, in 1861, thousands of veiled Persian women cou-
rageously broke the boundaries of their seclusion in the harem to sur-
round the carriage of the Shah, demanding action against the
government officials who were profiteering during a famine.[46]
Women played a leading and conspicuous role in the food riots in rev-
olutionary Paris in 1789, and in England where such riots periodically
erupted in the seventeenth and eighteenth centuries. In the United
States in the 1960s, it was women in the urban ghettos who joined in
a protest movement to demand that the "relief system" provide
greater benefits for food, rent, and clothing.[47] In the 1980s grandmothers, mothers, and daughters converged on Washington, D.C.,
from often remote and traditionally conservative parts of the country
to march together in unprecedented numbers to protest legislative
restrictions on abortion rights.

Women use public space to protest against violence in all its poi-
sonous forms: starvation, poverty, illness, homelessness, urban blight,
rape, abortion control, pornography, homophobia, the indignity suf-
fered by the differently abled and older people, racism, sexism, the
depletion of the earth's riches, the fouling of her air and water, the
arms race, imperialism. Women do so because they understand that
all of these are connected. Women march in defiance of male boundaries. As Virginia Woolf wrote: "As a woman, I have no country; as a
woman, my country is the world."[48] Feminism, in its fullest meaning,

enjoins the human race to establish zones of liberation, and literally to reshape the territorial definition of our patriarchal world, along with the social identities and injustices that those boundaries have defined for all of us.

NOTES

1. Marge Piercy, "An Open Letter," in *Take Back the Night: Women on Pornography,* ed. Laura Lederer (New York: WIlliam Morrow, 1980), 7.

2. Yi-Fu Tuan, *Topohilia,* 220.

3. Lederer, introduction, *Take Back the Night,* 18.

4. John Berger, *Ways of Seeing* (Harmondsworth, England: BBC and Penguin, 1972), 45–47.

5. Nancy Henley, *Body Politics* (Englewood Cliffs: Prentice Hall, 1977); Anita Nager and Yona Nelson-Shulman, "Women in Public Places," *Centerpoint* 3, no. 3/4, issue 11 (Fall/Spring 1980): 145.

6. Nager and Nelson-Shulman, "Women in Public Places," 146.

7. Ardener, "Ground Rules and Social Maps," 33.

8. "British Women Decry Rape Penalties," *New Women's Times,* May 1982, 10.

9. "Rape Victim Jailed in Refusal to Testify Against Defendant," *New York Times,* 26 June 1986, A19.

10. Elizabeth W. Markson and Beth B. Hess, "Older Women in the City," *Signs* 5, no. 3, supplement (Spring 1980): 134.

11. Ibid., 134–35.

12. For more information, write to METRAC at 158 Spadina Road, Toronto, Ontario M5R2T8, or telephone (416) 392-3135.TDD. Also refer to the Fall 1989/Winter 1990 *Women and Environments,* a special issue on urban safety.

13. *Women and Environments* (Spring 1986): 6.

14. Jane Midgley, *The Women's Budget,* 3d ed. (Philadelphia: Women's International League for Peace and Freedom, 1989), 16.

15. "Homeless in America," *Newsweek,* 2 January 1984, 15–17.

16. Jennifer Stern, "Serious Neglect: Housing for Homeless People with AIDS," *City Limits,* April 1989, 12.

17. Midgley, *Women's Budget,* 16.

18. Sarah Babb, "Women's Coalition: New Voices for Affordable Housing," *City Limits,* April 1989, 8.

19. Karin Stallard, Barbara Ehrenreich, and Holly Sklar, *Poverty in the American Dream* (Boston: South End Press, 1986).

20. "Homeless in America," *Newsweek,* 25.

21. Midgley, *Women's Budget,* 17.

22. "Homeless in America," *Newsweek,* 22–23.

23. Ibid., 23.

24. "Bush Budget Funds McKinney, Cuts Housing," *Safety Network, The Newsletter of the National Coalition for the Homeless* 8, no. 3 (March 1989): 3; ibid., no. 6 (June 1989): 1; and Midgley, *Women's Budget*, 16.

25. "Homeless in America," *Newsweek*, 23.

26. Ibid., 21.

27. Patricia King, "The Street Girls," *Newsweek*, 2 January 1984, 24.

28. Alan M. Beck and Philip Marden, "Street Dwellers," *Natural History* (November 1977): 85.

29. Ibid.

30. Babb, "Women's Coalition," 8.

31. Beck and Marden, "Street Dwellers," 81; and Ann Marie Rousseau, "Homeless Women," *Heresies* 2 (May 1977): 86, 88.

32. Senator Manfred Ohrenstein, "Help for the Homeless," *Legislative Report* (1981), unpaginated.

33. "Homeless in America" *Newsweek*, 21–22.

34. Sara Rimer, "The Other City: New York's Homeless," *New York Times*, 30 January 1984, 84.

35. Andrea Dworkin, "Pornography and Grief," in *Take Back the Night*, ed. Lederer, 286.

36. Kim Hirsch, "Guerrilla Tactics at Brown," *Ms.*, October 1983, 61; and Henley, *Body Politics*, 63.

37. Ann-Christine D'adesky, "Peace Camps: A Worldwide Phenomenon," *Ms.*, December 1983, 108.

38. Susan Pines, "Women Tie Up the Pentagon," *War Resisters League News*, no. 228, Jan.-Feb., 1982, 1, 8.

39. "New York City Peace Camp," *New Women's Times*, (September 1983): 20; and D'adesky, "Peace Camps," 108.

40. D'adesky, "Peace Camps," 108.

41. Carol Gilligan, *In a Different Voice* (Cambridge: Harvard University Press, 1982).

42. Ibid., 48–49; and Jean Baker Miller, *Toward a New Psychology of Women* (Boston: Beacon Press, 1976).

43. Gilligan, *In a Different Voice*, 38, 164, 174.

44. Sarah Charlesworth, "Ways of Change Reconsidered: An Outline and Commentary on Women and Peace in Northern Ireland," *Heresies* 2 (May 1977): 78–80.

45. Nell McCafferty, "Daughter of Derry," *Ms.*, Sept. 1989, 73, 76.

46. Elise Boulding, *The Underside of History* (Boulder, Colo.: Westview Press, 1976), 720.

47. Richard A. Cloward and Frances Fox Piven, "Hidden Protest: The Channeling of Female Innovation and Resistance," *Signs* 4, no. 4 (Summer 1979): 657.

48. Virginia Woolf, as quoted in D'adesky, "Peace Camps," 108.

4

The Home as Metaphor
for Society

If men control public space—from the street to the nation-state—do women control domestic space? No! The home also embodies a male/female territorial dichotomy, both symbolically and spatially. For example, the familiar cliché "a woman's place is in the home" and its complementary adage, "a man's home is his castle," have been submerged in the muddied waters of misuse for so long that many people fail to recognize what they really mean. Subsumed in these expressions is a complex set of deeply felt social relations in which men own and "rule" domestic space, while women are confined to and maintain it. Wherever there is social inequality, be it between women and men, black and white, or servant and served, the design and use of public space, public buildings, and domestic architecture will reflect it. Those with greater social status will spatially exclude those with lesser social status; and when "superior" and "inferior" groups do share space, they will not stand in the same relationship to it.

Domestic Space and Social Roles

Perhaps at no time in Western history was the home more celebrated as a repository for societal values than during the Victorian era, which gave rise to the cult of female domesticity. While home and work had been complementary to each other prior to the nineteenth century, comprising a unity of social existence for women and men, master and servant, by the mid-nineteenth century they had become two distinct and isolated spheres. The home and family provided a moral counterforce to the cut-throat individualism and ruthless economic ambition that characterized the newly industrialized society. The private house was designated a place of sanctuary, repose, and renewal in which the old values of security, stability, and cooperation could be safely enshrined. The highly sentimentalized figure of woman became the "guardian angel" of the house.

The Victorian wife and mother, endowed with love and gentleness, not energy and power, was banished from the public arena and confined to the domestic hearth where she could remain unsullied by the events of public life, maintain the tender virtues of kindness and selflessness, deter her husband from antisocial behavior, and reign on the "throne of the heart." Locked out from economic productivity, she assumed a spiritual role. For her, the home became both altar and prison, and her authority within it was exerted entirely by way of symbolism. For her husband, the home was indeed his "castle," a place in which his authority and rule were unquestioned, his control over family decisions absolute. Men were faced with the stress of an insecure job situation in which vast and impersonal corporations controlled their lives and livelihoods and success depended upon unpredictable market conditions, not personal skills. To escape the storms of a maturing but turbulent corporate capitalism they retreated to the snug harbor of the home.

Suburban domestic architecture embodied in both literal and symbolic ways the values of safety, privacy, and family that Americans craved during this period of urban conflict and dislocation. An apprehensive and uneasy population was attracted to eclectic styles like the Colonial Revival, reminiscent of a more secure past, homes surrounded by abundant foliage and landscaping to create the pastoral tone of the rural ideal, and homes with massive chimneys and hearths to "keep the home fires burning" with a spirit of inward grace.

Perhaps more than anyone else in the century, Catharine Beecher consecrated the American home as a spiritual realm and woman's exclusive domain, where she practiced her singular occupation: domesticity. Born in 1800 in East Hampton, Long Island, the daughter of a Calvinist minister, Beecher today is often remembered primarily as the sister of the abolitionist and author Harriet Beecher Stowe. But during her time the enormous success of her books *A Treatise on Domestic Economy* (1841), adopted as a school text, and *The American Woman's Home* (1869), written with Harriet Beecher Stowe, made her name a household word.[1]

Catharine Beecher was a woman of incredible intellect and energy, a pioneering teacher, writer, designer, and moral philosopher. Her domestic ideology supported female supremacy in the home based on two metaphorical roles of authority: the minister and the trained professional. Beecher viewed the home as a "Christian commonwealth" with woman as the ministerial head of the "home church of Jesus Christ." Through self-sacrifice, women could exert their religious and moral influence on their husbands and children, thereby influencing

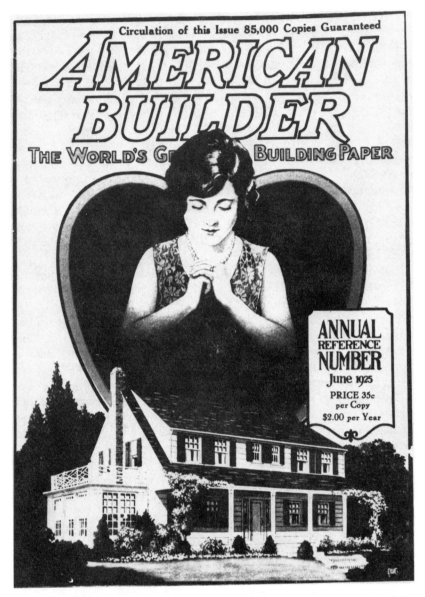

Figure 11. The Victorian notion of woman as the "guardian angel" of the sacred family house was used as a forceful device for promoting house sales during the Progressive Era, as depicted on this front cover of *American Builder* (1925), a magazine directed toward the building trades. Photograph by author.

the destiny of the nation. The parlor was to be the cultural podium from which women would indirectly exert political and social "power."

Beecher's domestic model of the "family state," based on exaggerated and dichotomized gender roles, sought to recreate the colonial family commonwealth which inextricably bound together the home, church, and government. Through the design and management of homes created by women, the "family state" would multiply across the land. In *The American Woman's Home* Beecher wrote: "In the divine word it is written 'the wise woman buildeth her house.' To be 'wise' is to choose the best means for accomplishing the best end. It has been shown that the best end for a woman is the training of God's children for their eternal home by guiding them to intelligence, virtue and true happiness. When therefore the wise woman seeks a home in which to exercise this ministry, she will aim to secure a house so planned that it will provide in the best manner for health, industry, and economy."[2]

Beecher's ideas about health, industry, and economy are conveyed in her books in technologically innovative and remarkably comprehensive designs. Foreshadowing the time and motion studies of home economists like Ellen Swallow Richards, Christine Frederick, and Lillian Moller Gilbreth between 1910 and 1930, she engineered streamlined counters, sinks, dumbwaiters, built-in cupboards, and movable, multipurpose wall storage units (see fig. 12). She carefully located kitchen windows to provide cross-ventilation and abundant sunlight, described the best-cooking stove, and evaluated the spatial organization of houses to determine the most efficient geometry, deciding that the perfect square was the most practical and least expensive shape for a home.[3] In her sample floorplans, the kitchen is centrally located to allow the "woman occupant" full visual control over the activities of the home without wasting time and energy walking back and forth.

Beecher also wrote an extremely long discourse on the scientific principles of conduction, convection, radiation, and reflection, arguing that healthful, beautiful homes resulted from proper site orientation, ventilation, and indoor plumbing (she felt out-houses caused "ill health"). "Owing to the ignorance of architects, house builders and men in general, they have been building school houses, dwelling houses, churches, and colleges with the most absurd and senseless contrivances for ventilation, . . . and all from not applying this simple principle of science."[4] Other topics she discussed included childrearing, budgeting, manners, nutrition, laundering, sewing, gardening, and mental and physical health.

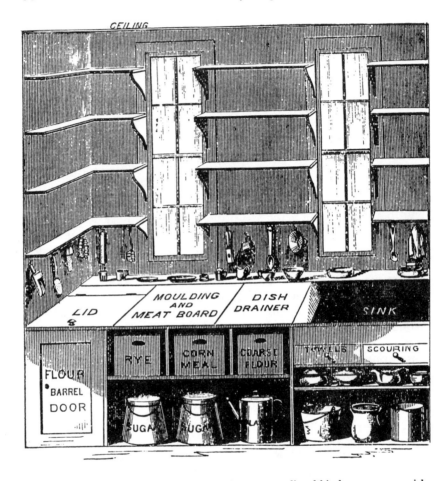

Figure 12. Catharine Beecher's design for a streamlined kitchen counter with built-in cupboards, shelves, storage bins, and sink. From Catharine Beecher and Harriet Beecher Stowe, *The American Woman's Home*, 1869. Reproduced courtesy the Stowe-Day Foundation, Hartford, Connecticut.

Beecher's obsession with educating women to domesticity originated in her belief that women were devalued because they were not trained for the complex and varied work involved in household management as men were trained for their respective professions. Therefore, she wrote, "The honor and duties of the family state are not duly appreciated" and "family labor is poorly done, poorly paid, and regarded as menial and disgraceful."[5] She supported her argument by a most unusual economic rationalization. Since servants were increasingly difficult to obtain as the factory system enticed the working-class population away from domestic employment, women would do their own work, thereby fulfilling their dual role as self-sacrificing spiritual minister and skilled professional. Homemaking, she reasoned, was an ideal occupation for women of all classes because it would "confer purpose on the aimless vacuity of rich women, ennoble the unrequited toil of poor women, as well as improve the prestige of middle class women."[6]

Catharine Beecher's impact as a domestic economist was far reaching. While her inventiveness and scholarship were undeniably impressive, the sexism inherent in her sex-stereotyping of household work and her fusion of self-sacrifice with capitalist material culture continues in the ongoing belief that women, whether they work outside the home or not, are responsible for domestic work.

The separate physical spheres of "man's world," "woman's place" that Catharine Beecher and her era fostered created a change in the quality of relationships between women and men. The implicit sexual symmetry and instinctive sharing of premodern society were replaced with a formal, contrived partnership in which the sexes joined together from opposite directions. Neither understood the other's daily existence, and character itself seemed gender-specific, either "masculine" or "feminine." Single-sex clubs proliferated and household space was organized to reflect the separate worlds and identities of women and men.

Consider, for example, the epitome of the Victorian home, the English country manor house (circa 1850–70)—by no means a typical home, but an idealized version—a microcosm of society offering a clear illustration of how relations between the sexes were to be arranged. Interior space was elaborately differentiated according to a careful "sociosexual code." The drawing and morning rooms "belonged" to the women, the smoking and billiard rooms to the men. The conservatory, reserved for the cultivation of exotic plants and the courtship of young couples, was located socially between these poles. The spatial segregation of the sexes in the respective domains of the male butler and female housekeeper was also rigorously enforced. Further, segregated staircases and hallways were designed to avoid chance encounters between the sexes, and between the servants and those whom they served. Floorplans typically include a divided "principal staircase," "bachelor's staircase," "young ladies' stair," "women's stair" for female servants, and "back stair" for male servants.

American gentry, the self-made millionaires who became the "captains of industry" in the nineteenth century, lived in similar, albeit "smaller" versions of the English country house. The Newport, Rhode Island, oceanfront summer "cottages" designed by the fashionable architect Richard Morris Hunt—such as Marble House, built in 1892 for William K. Vanderbilt, and the Breakers, built in 1895 for Cornelius Vanderbilt to resemble a sixteenth-century Italian palace—inevitably included separate rooms for each sex: richly paneled billiard rooms and libraries for the gentlemen, gilded morning rooms and boudoirs for the ladies.

By the turn of the century and during the first quarter of the twentieth century, the home was firmly established as a spatial metaphor for gender roles; and the ruling social and architectural elite in America were still reinforcing this prevailing standard. Further, the "servant problem" continued to be debated. Qualified servants were increasingly hard to find. The number of persons employed in household service in the country dropped from 1,851,000 in 1910 to 1,411,000 in 1920, while the number of households rose from 20.3 million to 24.4 million.[7] In addition, unpaid family workers such as daughters and maiden aunts were finding jobs "downtown." An examination of architectural house plans shows that maids' rooms were disappearing and kitchens were being designed for housewives, not servants.

In 1934, Frank Lloyd Wright designed the Malcolm Willey house in Minneapolis, with the "first" kitchen that was not a separate room. The open floorplan that became associated with his name emphasized family togetherness. Wright usually made the entire first floor a single large space that merged living, dining, and other common rooms, separating activities by screens and suggestion rather than walls and doors. In his scheme, mothers were not isolated in their kitchens from other family members (as servants had been), and children at play could be supervised.

Wright was a staunch supporter of the American family. The civic and social demands of the turn-of-the-century city weakened kinship ties and threatened family stability, especially among the middle class. Fathers spent their days at work, mothers involved in voluntary organizations, and children at school or with playmates. Wright's flowing interior space brought family members physically together more often, allowing them to be seen and making their presence felt throughout the house.[8]

Another avid supporter of keeping the traditional family together through the symbolic imagery and literal organization of the house was Emily Post, a socialite and the author of the *Blue Book of Etiquette*. While Post is best known for her writing on social conduct, her

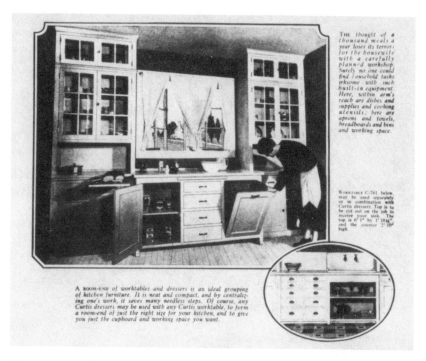

THE thought of a thousand meals a year loses its terrors for the housewife with a carefully planned workshop. Surely no one could find household tasks irksome with such built-in equipment. Here, within arm's reach are dishes and supplies and cooking utensils; here are aprons and towels, breadboards and bins and working space.

WORKTABLE C-761, below, may be used separately or in combination with Curtis dressers. Top is to be cut out on the job to receive your sink. The top is 6' 1" by 1' 10¼", and the counter 2' 10" high.

A ROOM-END of worktables and dressers is an ideal grouping of kitchen furniture. It is neat and compact, and by centralizing one's work, it saves many needless steps. Of course, any Curtis dressers may be used with any Curtis worktable, to form a room-end of just the right size for your kitchen, and to give you just the cupboard and working space you want.

Figure 13. During the 1920s and the 1930s, American builders promoted sales of building products and home appliances, particularly for the kitchen, by illustrating how a well-designed, efficient home would transform housework from drudgery into a manageable and pleasurable challenge, thereby improving the housewife's status and the quality of her family life. This advertisement from a 1926 Curtis Woodwork brochure proclaims, "The thought of a thousand meals a year loses its terrors for the housewife with a carefully planned workshop." Photograph by author.

contribution to the enforcement of gender roles was considerable. In 1930, Post published *The Personality of a House*, a book that became so popular it was reprinted almost annually until 1939, and again in 1948.[9]

Just as Americans were eager to learn proper manners, they also wanted to know what constituted the "proper" kind of house, and Post obliged by describing a very different set of spaces and esthetic criteria for women and men. Post called for a special "man's room" in every home to comfort and reassure the family (see fig. 14). "All rooms of dignity and untrimmed simplicity are suitable for a man," wrote Post. A man's room, "first of all, must look as though it were

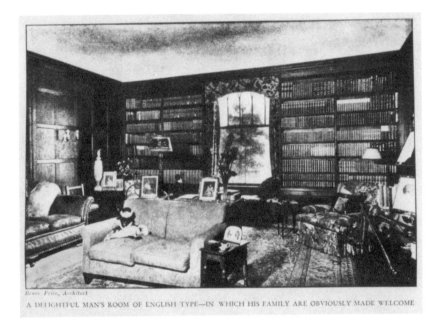

Bruce Price, Architect

A DELIGHTFUL MAN'S ROOM OF ENGLISH TYPE—IN WHICH HIS FAMILY ARE OBVIOUSLY MADE WELCOME

Figure 14. "The kind of room a man likes," said Emily Post, should be "unspoilable," "comfortable," "dignified," "simple," in other words, essentially practical and usable. The man's room shown here includes the recommended "well-filled book shelves" to reflect intelligence, a high ceiling which "makes a room masculine to begin with," and the use of family portraits as decorative objects, among his other "personal possessions." From Emily Post, *The Personality of a House*, 1930. Reproduced courtesy Elizabeth Post.

used. It must, moreover, be obviously comfortable, restful, quietly pleasing. . . . It may be a workshop, perhaps it is principally a place for him and his friends to smoke in after dinner, perhaps it is an office, perhaps it is a room where its owner can go off by himself to rest or to think." She recommended that every man's room include a fireplace and substantial, upholstered furniture, and exclude children and unwelcome guests. Post cautioned that it was "only natural that any normal man should be repelled by the least suggestion of effeminacy . . . " and warned decorators to avoid "chairs that look easily breakable, coverings light and perishable in color and texture, all the things that go to the making of feminine rooms. . . . " In short, a man's room must reflect his right to comfort, privacy, and individual self-expression.[10]

While Post designed rooms for men based on what they do and

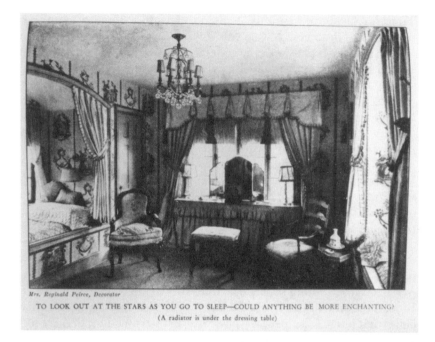

Mrs. Reginald Peirce, Decorator

TO LOOK OUT AT THE STARS AS YOU GO TO SLEEP—COULD ANYTHING BE MORE ENCHANTING?
(A radiator is under the dressing table)

Figure 15. "Feminine rooms," advised Emily Post, should include "delicate furniture, ornate fabrics, and pastel colors"; in other words, they should be essentially decorative and easily perishable. In this example of a "feminine bedroom," the prominent dressing table with its large mirror and assorted cosmetics and perfumes emphasizes a woman's sensuality. From Emily Post, *The Personality of a House*, 1930. Reproduced courtesy Elizabeth Post.

who they are, she designed rooms for women based on how they look (see fig. 15). She instructed women to choose surroundings that were personally "becoming" rather than detracting from their appearance. She divided women into three "types"—"blondes, brunettes, and mediums." Just as the "noonday blonde [the Marilyn Monroe 'type'] must be careful to stay slim or she will become too full-blown," wrote Post, "she must choose surroundings of distinction and simplicity or she will make them as well as herself look tawdry. Therefore, she must assiduously avoid robin's-egg blue; true, this is usually her favorite color, but it exaggerates rather than becomes her."

Post believes the "moon blonde" ("the porcelain doll") was best suited to rooms that were so "fragilely feminine" that her husband "should have a plain wood-lined room to counterbalance the rooms that are too obviously hers." Post cautioned, "Let him not have heavy

Tudor or Jacobean furniture if she is to be admitted, ever." She continued: the "drab blonde (the 'all-American girl') fits into the sort of
house that a man likes with the suitability of a boy." Her surroundings
should reflect warm, "homelike qualities that attract"—knotty pine,
small-patterned chintz, reds, oranges, and yellows. She advised the
"stay-at-home mother of many children . . . whose hands and
thoughts are chiefly occupied with her husband and children" always
to consider two prime qualities in her surroundings: cheerfulness to
please her husband and unspoilability to keep her children from ru-
ining everything in sight.[11]

To Post, the home was literally an extension of its occupants' personalities: "The house that does not express the individuality of its
owner is like a dress on a wax figure."[12] Like Catharine Beecher, Post
promoted the home as a spiritual domain whose beauty and charm
originated, as in people, not from external appearance but from an
internal soul. She wrote: "The charm of a house, like the charm of a
person, is an outward manifestation of inward grace. Artificially applied, it is like nothing so much as rouge on an old woman's cheeks."[13]
Indeed the title of her book, *The Personality of a House*, expresses her
belief that homes, like people, have different personalities that are lik-
able or disagreeable: "a room can be every bit as rude as a person."[14]

Further, Post endows the house with human attributes and qualities that are biological as well as psychological. Parts of the house are
analogous to body parts. Windows smile or grimace. Front doors are
hands: "A hideously untidy door is like a dirty hand that is repellent
to touch."[15] Houses, like people, have different physical constitutions;
they can be healthy or unhealthy: "Whether there is any truth in the
fear that houses, like children, will 'catch their death' unless kept off
the damp grass, I don't know; but I do know from very long experience that the more conscientious the mason or carpenter, the more
surely will he stand a building on its tiptoes—on stilts—if he has
his own way. The more surely, too, will he carry up the roof until
it perches far above the eyebrows, like a woman's hat of the gay
nineties."[16]

Post viewed the house as a living being that must be treated with
the same sensitivity and care as any other member of the family. She
reveals her obsession with family unity in a chapter called "The Principles of Color Harmony," in which she explains color schemes for
home decoration through the following metaphor: "The safest recipe
for harmony is to keep within the immediate family section as marked
by each of those boundaries . . . the sister of green is married to blue.

Blue's brother is married to violet. Violet's sister to red. But red is married to yellow and orange is one of their children. . . . But just as the families within the enclosures are in undisturbable accord, the nearest neighboring cousins on either side of the barriers are discords. Red-orange and red-violet fight like Kilkenny cats. . . . "[17]

Emily Post's translation of masculine and feminine stereotypes and family harmony into home decoration can best be understood in historical context. Post published her book one year after the stock market crash of 1929 that signaled the Great Depression. Further, like most Americans, she was deeply moved by the repercussions of World War I in which the lives of so many men were lost. She associated the modern style of her day (art moderne/art deco) with death and tragedy: "We feel the subconscious aftermath of the Great War translated into the rounded edges of highly polished, massively plain rectangles of ebony darkness, suggestive of coffins—even to the silver handles. . . . only in rare examples is it beautiful; and more rarely still can it by any stretch of the imagination be called homelike."[18] Her book promotes home design that creates the illusion of security and family stability through traditional styles and symbols of a strong and active male presence and a dependent and passive female counterpart.

About a decade later, Dorothy Field, in *The Human House* (1939), added to Post's guidelines on how "tasteful" American homes should look and function by cataloguing different domestic spaces according to their respective uses and meanings for each family member; for example:

> Father's point of view:
> a place to rest up after work
> a place to entertain
> a workshop for a hobby
> a private study . . .
>
> Mother's point of view:
> a place to work and to show
> a work place for cooking, sewing, washing and ironing
> nursery space for teaching walking, talking,
>   eating, climbing, hanging up clothes,
>   dressing and undressing
> a habit training center for school and
>   adolescent children
> a family community center for fun
> equipment for care of family's health
> storage space for family property. . . . [19]

Father, who works in the public marketplace, is given space of his own for privacy, personal pleasure, and leisure pursuits. For him, the house is still a place of renewal. For mother, private space and the status, adulthood, and sense of individuality it affords are glaringly absent. For her, the house is still her "boundary," her "sphere," and a never-ending, specialized workplace devoted to the growth, development, and fulfillment of other family members.

By the 1950s, standards of homemaking and motherhood effectively ensured that the conscientious American housewife would remain housebound. Throughout the nineteenth and twentieth centuries the invention of new household appliances did ease the physical burden of household work but, concomitantly, new jobs were created that took up as much time as those they replaced. Ruth Schwartz Cowan's research on the "industrial revolution" in the home documents this phenomenon. For example, in the 1920s the average housewife had fewer children than her mother, but standards of childcare required her to do things for her children her mother never dreamed of, such as preparing infant formula, sterilizing baby bottles, planning nutritionally well-balanced meals, having frequent consultations with teachers, and driving children to music and dance lessons. The consumption of economic goods offers another example of how the housewife's responsibilities expanded in the 1920s as home economists began to teach housewives how to shop properly and spend money wisely on the "best" products—in short to be informed consumers.[20]

The point of these examples is summarized in research by JoAnn Vanek surveying studies of the time that unemployed housewives spent on household work. She concluded that the time remained constant throughout the period 1920-70.[21] Women have continuously been pressured by "rising" standards and changing definitions of domesticity to remain endlessly engaged in cleaning, laundering, cooking, and the tending of young children in isolation from other adults, to the point at which, during the 1950s, female self-worth seemed directly related to the ability to fashion a clown's face out of fruit slices in a jello mold.

Further, a 1972 study by Irwin Altman et al. revealed that American mothers still lacked spatial and psychological privacy within the house. Their "special rooms," such as the kitchen, remained public places associated with the care and maintenance of others, while American fathers continued to claim and control their own private studies and workshops.[22] This principle of male privilege applies to those who live in less than the middle- and upper-class affluence the presence of a private study suggests. Working-class husbands and fathers also retain their place at the "head of the table" and their children are instructed never to sit in "Daddy's lounge chair."

Throughout the 1970s, hopes that domestic liberation was at last in sight ran high among women whose lives had been profoundly changed by the women's movement. Finally, men would assume their fair share of household responsibilities and parenting as equal partners with women. During that decade, and in the 1980s, women sought paid employment—out of personal choice and economic necessity—in unprecedented numbers. Today it is widely accepted, if not expected, that most women will work outside the home at some time, with perhaps occasional time off for childbearing. For the majority of women who are self-supporting and for those whose paychecks are an essential contribution to household income, time off from work for any reason is a "luxury" they cannot afford.

To what extent has women's changed employment pattern altered the domestic environment and women's traditional relationship to it? Very little. While the microwave oven may have made cooking dinner faster, women are still doing most of the cooking. Whether employed or not, most women still take care of the children, increasingly as single mothers and daycare providers; whether coupled or single, they still do the brunt of the housework, in their own homes and as paid housekeepers in the homes of others. In a poll conducted by the *New York Times* in June and July 1989, 62 percent of women between the ages of thirty and forty-four—the group who came of age at the height of the women's movement, agreed with the statement, "Most men are willing to let women get ahead, but only if women do all the housework at home." In a longitudinal study of "working parents and the revolution at home" published in 1989, Arlie Hochschild computed that American women in the past two decades have worked roughly fifteen hours longer each week than men. Over a year, that adds up to an extra month of twenty-four-hour days.[23] As in past eras, the "job description" for "women's work" has simply been expanded.

Domestic Violence:
A Private Family Affair

Just as men have historically owned and ruled their homes, the legal and religious institution of marriage has traditionally guaranteed to them the ownership and control of wives and children as property. Even though we like to think of the home as a nurturing place and the relationships within it as loving and supportive, scenes of domestic violence, both physical and psychological, are enacted daily behind the door of the private family house.

An estimated twenty-eight million American wives are battered by their husbands each year, almost half of all married women in the country. The FBI claims that an incident of wife abuse occurs every fifteen seconds, making it America's most common crime.[24] But the familiar term "wife abuse" is misleading. Women are also battered by fathers and boyfriends, prostitutes by pimps and sadistic customers, elderly mothers by their grown sons (a phenomenon known as "granny bashing"), and lesbians coming out of heterosexual relationships by the men they leave. The problem is world wide.

Historically, the police have been reluctant to intervene in a scene of domestic violence, a fact partially explained by the social beliefs that a home is a "man's castle" and interference in private family "spats" is wrong. They have been trained to make every effort to keep the family unit together—an approach that keeps a battered woman in a very dangerous environment.

Women who suffer domestic abuse are trapped in their homes by an agonizing fear of the batterer, their own inability to survive financially without him, and shameful social attitudes that hold the victim responsible for her abuser's behavior. Understandably, many women hide their injuries, stay at home until the bruises fade, or, if medical attention is needed, claim to have had a "household accident." Boston City Hospital reports that 70 percent of the assault victims treated in its emergency room are women who have been attacked by a husband or lover in their homes.[25] Richard Gelles determined that scenes of violence are most frequently enacted in the kitchen, followed by the bedroom and living room. Sometimes battles progress from one room to another. The only room in which Gelles found no violence was the bathroom.[26]

Other studies of homicide show that the bedroom is the deadliest room in the house and the victims there are most often women. When family murders occur in the kitchen, traditionally women's "territory," the victims are most often men. In assault cases that end in death, wives are predominantly the victims; in homicides, husbands are victims almost as often as wives, explained by the fact that women who commit murder are motivated by self-defense seven times as often as are male offenders.[27] While women are often advised to "stay home where they won't get hurt," these statistics imply that women are less safe in their own homes than they are in the streets.

When patriarchal violence becomes a household pattern, it is often visited through women upon children. In her desperation, the battered wife may strike out at her child not only by battering, but by manipulating, cajoling, and inducing guilt. Children who witness violence between parents suffer serious emotional trauma, and they often beat or are beaten as adults, passing the violence from one generation to another like some inevitable and immutable law of nature. The breaking point for many abused women comes when they fear for their children's safety.

For most women, escape from domestic violence depends upon the existence of places of safety that they can turn to for help. During the 1970s, feminists began to create shelters for battered women and their children and sought legislation that would reform the American family court system so that it could immediately intervene when a woman felt she was in danger of attack by her husband. Today, a battered woman (without a lawyer) may file a court complaint mandating a restraining order against her abuser, seven days a week; and the violation of a court order is now a felony. If she needs medical treatment, an officer must take her wherever she needs to go. Police protection must be available until her safety is ensured. Domestic violence must now be treated as would any crime not involving household members.

But the need for places of refuge for battered women and their children is no less desperate today than it was in 1971 when Erin Pizzey and a few supporters established an "advice center" in London, England. The center was supposed to be a place where married women could escape loneliness and meet to discuss their mutual concerns. But an overwhelming majority of those who came were battered women, who previously had nowhere to go. The center developed into the Chiswick Women's Aid, popularly known as the Battered Wives Center.

Wherever shelters were and are established, the problems remain the same. Money is inevitably the biggest obstacle; without it, finding, buying, renovating, and maintaining space is next to impossible. With paltry funding, the physical conditions in most shelters vary from shabby to shameful. Overcrowding remains a critical problem. Shelters are always filled to capacity and beyond. For example, in Chicago, in 1984, over 400 battered women were turned away each month from the ten shelters that are in operation. Estimates are that 700 shelters would have been required in that year to meet the needs of abused women in just that city alone. In 1989 approximately 350

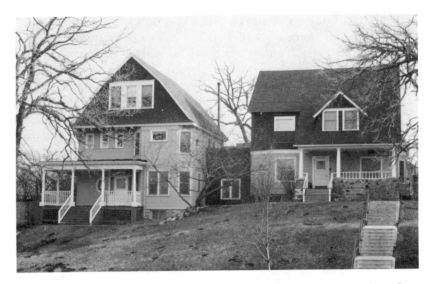

Figure 16. Women's Advocate's Shelter, St. Paul, Minnesota, 1988. View of exterior showing the two renovated houses linked together. Photograph courtesy Mary Vogel, architect.

shelters were operating in the United States, about one-half the required number according to the National Coalition Against Domestic Violence, which reports that shelters nationwide receive 50 percent more requests than they can handle.[28]

The legal, economic, social, political, and architectural aspects involved in creating shelters for women are complex. The history of the Women's Advocate's Shelter in St. Paul, Minnesota, provides an instructive example of their interplay. The shelter opened in a large, single-family Victorian house at 584 Grand Street on 12 October 1974. After years of operation in crowded conditions, the shelter's operators purchased the house next door at 588 Grand Street to expand the size of the facility. The renovation, completed in 1981 and financed partially with $450,000 substantial rehabilitation subsidies by the U.S. Department of Housing and Urban Development, linked the two houses together to create emergency housing for twenty-eight people (see figs. 16 and 17), although the shelter has continuously accommodated forty residents at a time.[29]

The first floor contains a communal kitchen, dining room, lounge, and children's room, a bedroom for handicapped residents, and the intake office. The link between the two houses serves as a seating area that allows mothers to see their children at play outside. The second

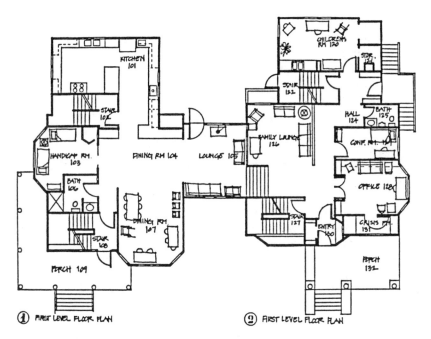

Figure 17. The first-floor plan of the Women's Advocate's Shelter, St. Paul, Minnesota. Drawing courtesy Julia W. Robinson.

floor houses the residents in private bedrooms with shared bathrooms. Additional "apartments," along with administrative offices, are on the third floor. The basement contains storage, laundry, mechanical equipment, and children's play spaces.

In many ways it would have been easier to design and build a new structure. But the Women's Advocate's Shelter recognized the intrinsic homelike beauty of the two houses and feared this quality would be lost in a new building that would have to adhere to institutional codes. Further, the houses' compatibility with the existing neighborhood contributed to the neighbors' acceptance of the shelter, an important asset that a new structure might jeopardize.

The decision to renovate meant that the architect, Mary Vogel, had to reconcile restrictive institutional safety codes with the two wood-frame residential structures, which resulted in certain problems. For example, the four required enclosed fire staircases took up a large amount of space and looked very institutional. To offset their appearance, Vogel installed carpeting, which presented a maintenance problem. Another example is the difficulty created by the required use of heavy metal fire doors throughout the staircases, which made entering and exiting awkward for mothers carrying laundry and children.

The architect also had to find room for a number of families and support personnel to live and work in buildings originally designed to house two separate families. The overall environment had to afford the residents and staff their privacy without creating a sense of isolation, and foster but not force opportunities for human contact and interaction. Making the shelter accessible to disabled women required considerable design ingenuity.

The "image" of the shelter was especially important. It had to look like a home, because it was acting as one, but it also had to look secure to suggest its purpose as a refuge. Further, it had to be secure to protect residents from unwanted intruders. It is not unusual for angry men to pursue their partners and children. (Although most shelters try to keep their addresses secret for as long as possible, their locations inevitably become known.) Trespassers must be visible, visitors identified, and entrance and exit points secure. Yet no one wants to live in a prison. Battered women are victims, not criminals.

There are many conflicts inherent in creating security in a place for family living. Outdoor night lighting that floods the property aids security but sacrifices the homelike atmosphere. Unlocked doors make residents and staff nervous; locked doors are difficult in an open family environment. The staff has to make endless trips to answer the door as residents come and go.[30]

The regulation of cigarette smoking creates another conflict between the safety requirements of an institution and the personal freedom of being "at home." Smoking causes problems of fire safety and infant health, but it eases tension and helps pass the time. In shelters, women who were casual smokers often become heavy smokers. For most residents the rules that prohibit smoking in the bedrooms mean that bedrooms cannot be used as comfortable, private retreats. But the need to protect resident safety in sleeping areas takes precedence. Like other conflicts, the resolution of the smoking question involves trade-offs.[31]

While the constraints of code regulations and budget did not permit the full realization of all their social and architectural ideals, the staff members of the Women's Advocate's Shelter are pleased with the design and workmanship of their building. However, they are disappointed about the poor quality of many of the building materials used in their house (and in most house construction today). Although they purchased the most durable products they could afford, they are nevertheless faced with constant repairs and replacement of the hardware on fire doors, closets, and kitchen cabinets; the doors themselves; and the walls. Between 1974 and 1989, the shelter housed over twelve thousand women and children; during those fifteen years, the staff has had to turn away three times that number—some thirty-six thousand women in need.[32]

Shelters for women exist today in many countries because of the energy, endurance, and devotion of countless women who know these facilities are urgently needed. Del Martin wrote in *Battered Wives* (1976), "I have reached the conclusion that the creation of shelters designed specifically for battered women is the only direct, immediate and satisfactory solution to the problem of wife abuse."[33] Like famine, flood, and earthquake, marital abuse is a social disaster that leaves millions of its victims—women and children—in need of protection, food and shelter, advice and emotional support. The women who work to provide it are deeply motivated by a philosophy of sisterhood that commits them to seeing other women's problems as their own, to recognizing personal problems as public issues, and to imagining a world in which women are not beaten, raped, mutilated, possessed, or controlled.

Public Housing: The Female Ghetto

Wife battering and child abuse—secrets swept quietly under the rug and locked safely away in the closets of millions of family homes—are the results of a society in which women and children "belong" to men. The prevalence of female-headed households in public housing is the result of a society in which women and children have the least. While the privately owned house symbolizes the stature of the traditional, male-headed family, American public housing serves the opposite purpose, that of segregating and stigmatizing poor, female-headed, primarily minority families. In 1980, 73 percent of American households in public housing were headed by women, and the figures were comparable in Canada.[34] By the late 1980s, the U.S. figure had risen to above 90 percent. Women are segregated in public housing because they are too poor to live anywhere else. In 1978 almost half of all female-headed households in America lived in poverty, compared to 5 percent of male-headed households.[35] Since then, poverty has decreased among families with men in them, but substantially increased in those headed by women. By the year 2000 virtually all the poor in America will be women and children, according to the National Advisory Council on Economic Opportunity.[36]

Because women are frequently more impoverished than men, in 1974 there was a 20 percent probability that a poor woman who headed a household would live in substandard housing, compared to 10 percent among the general population. If she was Hispanic as well, the probability increased to 26 percent; for black women it was 28 percent; among rural elderly women, whose geographic isolation makes them perhaps the least visible and most forgotten, 31 percent.[37] These statistics reflect the cruel consequences of interlocking gender, race, and class oppression.

The extent to which American women of diverse racial backgrounds are unable to find adequate shelter, and therefore depend on public housing, is a bitter comment on the prevalence of women's poverty. With the exception of the Federal Housing Administration (FHA) and the Veteran's Administration (VA) programs, federal housing programs are essentially women's programs. Even government-assisted housing for the "elderly" serves a predominantly female constituency, since the majority of older Americans are women and a disproportionate number of them are poor (see chapter 5).

Yet public housing was not created for low-income women. Quite the contrary. It was originally built as family housing for the "deserving poor"—i.e., parents and several children, who had been temporarily impoverished during the Great Depression in the 1930s. Gradually the definition of deserving "family" was enlarged to include first, the single elderly in the 1950s, and then, single disabled persons. However, the majority of single people remain ineligible for occupancy in public housing or for other government shelter subsidies such as Section 8, which pays the difference between 25 to 30 percent of a person's gross income and a monthly rent. Eligibility is thus defined on the basis of marital status, and concomitantly "proof" of one's heterosexuality. This is clearly unacceptable. Low-income housing should be available to anyone with a low income.

This housing policy is in effect a form of social control that supports and reinforces the patriarchal family. Canada, Australia, and the United Kingdom have similar policies and practices. One Canadian study found that half of all the women heading families in public housing had moved into the projects when they were living with their husbands because they felt being married would give them a better chance of getting in. They delayed marital breakdown until after the family had received a placement.[38] In Britain, the intact, working-class family is given preference in Council (government subsidized) housing.[39] In Australia, the largest public housing authority, the Housing Commission of New South Wales, has systematically discriminated against single persons who are not aged or disabled, even though that practice contravenes state government antidiscrimination legislation.[40]

What does the public housing that is home to millions of female-headed households cost the American government? Not much. Indeed, the government does spend billions of dollars each year on housing; but not housing for poor people. In 1988, direct spending on federal low-income housing assistance programs was $13.9 billion. In that same year, federal tax breaks (known as tax expenditures) for homeowners who paid mortgage interest and property taxes totaled $53.9 billion. In fact, the amount of tax expenditures for 1988 and 1989 ($107.4 billion) was almost equal to the amount spent on all low-income subsidized housing programs during the 1980s ($107.7 billion).[41] Those who benefit the most from government housing subsidies are not those with the greatest financial need, but those whose way of life conforms to the American "ideal."

Public housing has a bad reputation in America. No one, not welfare recipients or those with the lowest incomes, wants to live in a "project" built for "broken families" and "poor people." Such housing would logically be scorned in a society that equates poverty, divorce, and the need for social assistance with personal failure and flaws in one's character. The mention of American public housing evokes images of vandalism, disregard for property, people who don't care about their children, and long, cold hallways. Despite the cruelty of this stigma, homelessness is crueler still. There are long waiting lists to get into public housing everywhere in the country.

Residents of public housing find their lives are strictly regulated by both the power of their public landlord and the architecture that was built for their "rehabilitation." Early public housing officials believed that a model environment could promote "American" values, good habits, and good citizenship, and could help poor families get on their feet again. Typical of the housing units endorsed by officials was the absence of storage space; poor people were not supposed to have many material possessions. When there were closets, doors were left off to reduce costs and encourage neatness. To ensure that adults would not share their rooms with infants, the parents' bedrooms were purposefully small.[42]

Still, much early public housing was well designed and well built. The reason? It enabled the government to put millions of unemployed men back to work during the Depression. There were fifteen million jobless in 1933 and one-third of them were skilled in the building trades.[43] Because President Roosevelt was more concerned with creating jobs than controlling construction costs, the public housing constructed under his Public Works Administration Program (PWA) was frequently of better quality and design than private housing. Angry builders and realtors argued that "tenement" occupancy in public housing would become so attractive that it would diminish the desire for private homeownership, the very foundation of the American way of life.[44] As a result, by the 1940s the poor were being housed in cheap, austere buildings whose construction costs were controlled by congressional regulations that prohibited the government from building housing projects with elaborate or expensive materials or design that cost more than the average dwelling unit built by a private builder.[45]

In the 1950s, public housing became "black housing." Urban renewal programs—slum clearance often called "Negro removal"—destroyed thousands of units of low-income, inner-city housing, replacing most of it with middle-income and luxury apartments. Left with no affordable place to go, a disproportionate number of blacks were forced to apply for subsidized housing. Housing officials shifted their focus from rehabilitating the "deserving poor family" to enforcing order among racial minorities.

A dramatic example is Pruitt-Igoe in St. Louis, designed in 1956 to house about fifteen thousand people in thirty-three eleven-story high-rise buildings (see fig. 18). The architect, Minoru Yamasaki, designer of New York's World Trade Center, depicted middle-class, happy, white mothers and well-behaved children in his sketches, rather than the black welfare mothers and teenagers who, in reality, became the residents. No childcare, shops, or recreation facilities were planned. Children fell from unguarded windows and were scalded on uninsulated steam pipes. The labyrinthine skip-stop corridor system provided refuge for muggers. Since there were no ground-level public toilets, children urinated in the elevators. A serious vacancy and vandalism problem developed, and it continued into the late 1960s despite belated and costly efforts by the authorities to provide social and support services. Unable to keep the buildings occupied, the government dynamited the three central blocks on 15 July 1972. By 1976, all the structures had been demolished.[46]

The failure of Pruitt-Igoe was not caused by badly designed architecture alone. Many residents, when interviewed, said it was the best

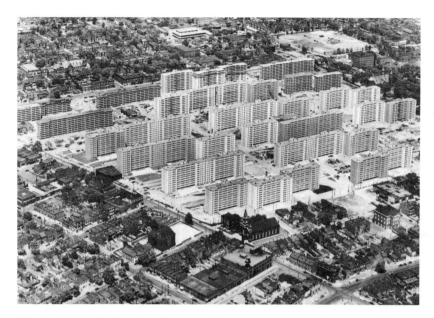

Figure 18. Pruitt-Igoe housing complex, St. Louis, Missouri, 1956, Minoru Yamasaki, architect. Photograph courtesy Bettmann Newsphotos–UPI, The Bettmann Archive, New York.

housing they had ever lived in. Rather, people chose not to live there because of the official public-housing policy of racism, ghettoization, and management brutality, combined with the fact that hundreds of thousands of houses in St. Louis became available, even for poor people, as over half of the city's white population left town between the time the projects were conceived and the time they were vacated.[47]

Massive, monotonous, and institutionalized high-rise projects like Pruitt-Igoe were built to identify the residents and isolate them from the surrounding neighborhoods. Functionalism and economy of scale were used as rationales. Long, dark hallways and exterior covered walkways became havens for crime. Thin walls made household privacy impossible. Quarrels and celebrations alike intruded upon neighbors. Rooms were small because occupants were supposed to use the huge, barren expanses of outdoor space. However, mothers kept their children indoors all day rather than leave them alone to play outside on the unsafe, empty concrete wastelands provided for them.

Without the means to secure childcare or transportation, mothers themselves were often unable to leave. The results: tension and overcrowding. One mother said, "You feel like you can't breathe. People are everywhere. Children are in the bathroom when you are using the toilet. Somebody is sitting in every chair in the house. You've got to eat in shifts."[48]

Residents of public housing are stripped of their privacy, choice, and often their dignity. Since the very beginning of public housing, management has exercised an abusive control over the residents' personal lives and activities. Although there has been a recent trend toward greater control by tenants, historically the policy about overnight guests, keeping pets, and hours in which to use washing machines, and the color of paint on the walls were all regulated.[49] (Ironically, in some luxury high-rises, similar rules are employed to create and maintain an elite aesthetic and social environment.)

Rules in public housing prohibit tenants from conducting any business on the premises, preventing women from establishing home childcare and earning money through "cottage industries" such as sewing or handicrafts. Residents must not earn more than a certain amount of money each month in order to live there. This is especially hard on women who do seasonal, contract, or piece work; for a few months their income may exceed the limit, but they may be unemployed for the next three. Nevertheless, their occupancy status is subject to review.

Household heads are required to show detailed reports of their incomes, and the names, ages, and relationships of other occupants. Failure to cooperate at any time could be grounds for termination of a lease. Any complaints about restrictions on personal freedom and activities can also result in a tenant's status being reviewed.[50]

Certainly minority women are not the only people to live with such conditions in public housing. Racism has ensured the relative poverty and powerlessness of minority males as well. But the fact that women and their children are the vast majority is evidence that, while some women's lives have improved as a result of the women's movement, other women's lives remain untouched and insufferable. The disadvantages that all women face when it comes to getting and maintaining shelter, whether public or private, owned or rented, are profoundly modified and shaped by a woman's economic class and race. The life of a welfare mother in a public housing development is altogether different from the life of a homemaker in suburbia, thwarted, frustrated, and oppressed as we now understand it to be.

In 1980, ten million women in America were living with leaking toilets, no heat or hot water, exposed electrical wiring, broken plaster, and peeling paint, with only the companionship of small children who are often hungry and always inadequately clothed. Today, many mothers stay awake all night to protect sleeping children from rats. Many other residents are old and frail. We read about them in the newspapers, found frozen to death in their own homes during severe winters.

It is not uncommon in American public housing to find garbage-lined hallways, elevators that reek of urine, and gangs of young men loitering in the trash-strewn yards making drug deals. Police and fire departments frequently refuse to enter these estates, and the discovery of fresh corpses in and around buildings—the victims of shootings and assaults—is a regular occurrence.

While the majority of residents in public housing feel outraged, frightened, depressed, and powerless in these conditions (for which they pay up to 40 percent of their monthly incomes as rent), some have turned their understandable anger and fear into an empowering catalyst for self-help solutions. At age nineteen, Kimi Gray was a divorced mother of five, living on welfare in Kennilworth Parkside, Washington, D.C., a 464-unit development housing three thousand people. In 1972, at age twenty-five, fed up living for three years with no heat or hot water, she got herself elected head of the development's residents' council. She and her council immediately organized tenants into committees, started cleanup brigades, appointed safety officers to keep the hall lights on and the front doors locked, and fostered a cooperative alliance between residents and the police. After Gray persuaded tenants not to buy stolen goods, burglaries plummeted. She organized tenant marches against neighborhood drug pushers and told resident pushers and addicts that if they did not quit in thirty days she would have them evicted. She encouraged residents to become active in the PTA (Parent-Teacher Association) at the local school and threatened to take some residents to court for neglecting their children. Gradually, the children's test scores began to rise.

In 1982 Kimi Gray and her colleagues negotiated with the District of Columbia for a total takeover of project management, maintenance, and governance by tenants. Today, Kennilworth Parkside is completely run by an elected resident board which received professional management training and now hires and fires it own staff. Kimi Gray is chair of the Kennilworth Parkside Resident Management Corporation, a multimillion dollar corporate enterprise whose accomplishments are impressive. By 1987, housing administration costs had been reduced by 60 percent; vacancy rates had fallen from 18 percent to 5.4 percent; welfare dependency among residents had been reduced from 85 percent in 1972 to 20 percent. Crime is down

90 percent and the rate of teenage pregnancy has been halved. Jobs for residents have been created in new businesses which include a screen-door repair shop, laundry, clothing boutique, catering company, health center, roofing company, moving company, snack bar and arcade center for youths, construction company, childcare center, food co-op store, and beauty shop. The ultimate goal of the residents is to purchase their homes and property, all twenty-six acres, and they plan to syndicate and develop a mortgage bank for this purpose. Much of the success at Kennilworth is attributed to Kimi Gray's "College Here We Come" program which, between 1975 and 1987, sent 582 youths to college. Today, graduates of the program serve as the architects, engineers, and lawyers who supervise the thirteen million dollar total modernization of Kennilworth properties.[51]

Similar successes in transforming blighted, public housing have been achieved in St. Louis. In 1969, twenty-year-old Bertha Gilke led a nine-month-long rent strike among some twenty-two thousand tenants in nine housing developments throughout the city to protest intolerable living conditions. In Cochran Gardens, her own housing development of twelve high-rise towers, there was so much vandalism that the housing authorities refused to install a coin laundry; snipers fired at pedestrians from the upper floors with such regularity that residents called the main building "Little Nam."

In 1975, Gilke went to the St. Louis Housing Authority and negotiated a management contract. The Cochran Tenant Management Corporation she formed turned those housing "projects"— once slated for demolition, like its neighbor Pruitt-Igoe—into high-quality developments equipped with swimming pools, playgrounds, and a community center, and resident owned and operated entrepreneurial ventures which have created hundreds of new jobs for residents in custodial, management, construction, security, childcare, catering, and chores for the elderly and disabled programs. Through joint ventures, Cochran Tenant Management Corporation has built seven hundred new townhouses for low- and moderate-income households and has plans for constructing a neighborhood shopping mall.[52]

Like Kimi Gray, Bertha Gilke sees homeownership as essential: "We have invested a lot of years and time in bringing these developments back up. . . . We're concerned that once we bring it back to standard, they will want it back like they always do. . . . We think homeownership is the only answer for poor people. They have to be in control of their community."[53] Contrary to the popular belief that women who live in public housing drain a city's resources, these two examples demonstrate the great potential that women have to revitalize and humanize cities, neighborhoods, and homes.

In addition to the achievements at Cochran Gardens and Kennilworth Parkside, in 1986 there were at least fourteen other public housing developments around America where residents had taken over some or all operating responsibilities, turning the forbidden concrete warrens into livable environments, in defiance of the stereotypical assumption by housing authorities that poor, uneducated people are incapable of self-management.[54] The "secret" of these successes is not architectural renovation, but rather human reeducation directed toward fostering self-esteem and efficacy. Tenant management corporations set tough standards for residents, levy fines for irresponsible behavior, screen applicants, have strong leadership and resident support, advocate for the rights afforded tenants in their leases, and launch early cleanup campaigns.

American public housing policies, established by policy "experts," have failed because they have invested money only in bricks and mortar, not in human beings. Deteriorating public housing and the broader social problems of the "underclass" must be addressed together in solutions that empower people with personal responsibility and control. Recently, the U.S. Department of Housing and Urban Development (HUD) created a Public Housing Homeownership Demonstration Program designed to meet this challenge by supporting tenant management in public housing and by helping residents to purchase their homes from the federal government by forming limited equity cooperatives. In 1989, HUD Secretary Jack Kemp called this program "chapter two of the civil rights movement."[55] Kemp's enlightened attitude and the goals of this new housing initiative are encouraging and essential if we are to make decent housing a reality for all Americans.

The dream of raising one's children in a decent place of one's own is no less compelling for women than men, for singles than couples, for the poor family than the rich one. Subsidized housing which fosters a debased social environment through its design, its management, or its social connotations is not a "gift" from society to the needy, it is at best tokenism and at worst a humiliating punishment.

A House Is Not A Home

Women's revolt against patriarchal injustice mandates the deconstruction of the family house that hides the housewife's isolation, the battered woman's pain, and the welfare mother's shame. If "the home" is to become a metaphor for a society based on human equality, dwellings must support and symbolize the valuing of our human diversity and difference. Equality does not mean "sameness." The image of the cozy bungalow surrounded by shade trees and a white picket fence may be fulfilling for some, but not for all.

In thinking about the home as a metaphor for society, it is important to understand the difference between the visual image and social meaning of a house as a physical object, a home as a social environment, and housing as an anonymous form of shelter. The private, "single-family" detached house is a sacred icon that embodies the "American dream." Americans have been led to aspire to and work toward owning their own house. With ownership comes adulthood, control over your own life, and full membership in mainstream society.

"Multifamily" housing, like rental apartments, is supposed to be for people in life transitions—singles who are not yet "settled down," young couples just starting out who need time to save a down payment on a house of their own, and older couples, "empty-nesters" who have sold their family houses and moved to smaller quarters with less responsibility to enjoy the earned rewards of retirement. Publicly subsidized housing, allegedly built to guarantee that no American would be homeless, has in reality served to isolate and stigmatize the poor—virtually all low-income minority women, single and welfare mothers, exiled from society for the crime of their poverty, the crime of living without husbands, and the crime of being nonwhite in a racist society. Children who grow up in the projects are made to feel ashamed every time they are asked for their addresses.

The type of physical dwelling and neighborhood in which one lives is heavily laden with emotional meaning, symbolizing a hierarchy of social status and social place. Where one lives influences how one sees oneself and others. And, regardless of the type of dwelling, women and men have been socialized to see their relationships to homes differently.

Men invest money in their homes; women invest their lives. While the home is certainly an important status symbol for both, for traditional housewives it can also become an intimate symbol of self. When a husband moves from the "family home" during a separation or divorce, though he may feel a deep loss, his personal identity, determined primarily through his job and workplace, will likely remain intact. When a wife loses her home through divorce or domestic abuse, she is likely, at least temporarily, to lose also her sense of self (an experience discussed in chapter 5).

Certainly in the last twenty years or so the conventional roles of the housewife and the male provider have changed dramatically. All one has to do to know this is true is to turn on a television set. Situation comedies portraying "new" kinds of households and "reversed" gender roles abound. As examples: in "Kate and Allie" two divorced mothers shared a house, the mortgage payments, and their problems with childraising; in "Who's the Boss" a "modern-day" widow and her corporate executive daughter share their house with a male housekeeper who is a single parent raising a teenaged daughter; in "The Cosby Show" the father of the family, a medical doctor, sees patients at home where he can also cook dinner and keep an eye on his children while his wife, a lawyer, is at work in her office; in "Full House" two men help a widowed father raise his two young daughters; in "Roseanne" a blue-collar couple who both work for wages struggle to make ends meet and raise their children; in "Dear John" a single male carries on with his life after a traumatic divorce; and in "The Golden Girls" four older women retire to Florida to share a home and companionship. These and countless other examples offer clear "evidence" of changing human identities in which both women and men of all ages can be independent, competent, domesticated, nurturing, wage earners, and responsible for raising children.

As the social boundaries of "woman's place" and "man's world" are reshaped, the meaning, use, and design of domestic space are also changing, albeit slowly and conservatively, particularly in terms of design. Understandably, architectural innovations are the most difficult to accomplish. They require considerable money, changes in zoning regulations and building codes, and the imagination and commitment of architects, builders, developers, and communities. (What is currently being done and could be done in the future is discussed in chapters 5 and 6.)

A Feminist Agenda for Housing and Community Design

The housing problems that many people are experiencing result from the ubiquitous sexism, racism, and classism that characterize patriarchal society. Housing, like affirmative action, reproductive freedom, or equal pay, belongs on the feminist agenda. Yet it is understandable that it has been added only recently—housing inequities are simply not as obvious as many of the other pressing problems women face. The now-illegal business practice of discounting a working wife's income in qualifying for a mortgage, based on the assumption that she would inevitably get pregnant and leave the labor force, could easily be perceived as a credit problem. Minority women can understandably blame racism, rather than sexism, for housing discrimination. For many women, housing problems are seen as economic problems—the result of job discrimination. But the case for ending the neglect of housing issues is strong and simple; shelter is crucial and women do not have equal access to it.

Those of us committed to social justice for women must not tolerate their systematic marginalization in the housing market. Because women are primarily renters with low incomes and therefore have little choice or control over their housing, we must demand that the American government establish a national housing allowance to provide financial relief and tenure security for all renters as it does with homeowners through tax deductions.[56] Homeownership is increasingly elusive and has never been viable for many American households. Apartments are also homes. Those who live in them must be guaranteed protection against prejudicial landlords, co-op and condominium conversions that threaten to displace low-income tenants, and the uncertainties of market fluctuations.

Because women are primarily responsible for children, we must support the implementation of recent national legislation that bans discrimination against children in rental housing. The nationwide paucity of rental units where children are accepted has reached crisis proportions as builders and landlords increasingly design and convert apartments to "adult-only" housing.[57] Certainly the consequences for families with children who cannot afford to buy a house are severe and often tragic, particularly among minority households, who frequently have more children and less income than white households. Families have been found living in abandoned buildings or cars; some find the stress of homelessness so great that they have placed their children in foster homes; and the U.S. Commission on Civil Rights is studying the correlation between housing discrimination against children and instances of child abuse and wife battering.[58] Any housing policy that excludes children will have the greatest exclusionary consequences for women, since they are the vast majority of millions of single parents. So-called "hysterectomy zoning" in the suburbs, designed to restrict apartment sizes and thereby hold down the school-age population, must be eradicated.

In March 1989 new amendments to the U.S. Federal Fair Housing Act (1968) became effective, with the intention of removing barriers to families with children in rental housing geared to singles and young adults. (The law recognizes that older people may have legitimate reasons for maintaining housing that is segregated by age and specifically exempts housing that includes significant services and facilities designed to meet the physical and social needs of older persons, such as health care, cooked meals, and recreation.) It is imperative that consumers be informed of their new rights and that advocates of fair housing monitor the funding and procedures needed for successful implementation of these important laws.

Because the majority of American women with children work for wages outside the home and have low to moderate incomes, high-quality, affordable public childcare must become an essential service, just as public schools are, and it should be a key element in housing and in urban and suburban planning. Further, we must establish laws that require developers of commercial office space to construct on-site childcare facilities within their developments or to contribute to a city-wide childcare fund that can be distributed to neighborhood facilities.[59]

Since those with low incomes are largely dependent upon public transportation to get to jobs, stores, or doctor's appointments, and since minority and elderly women comprise a large percentage of this group, we must insist that the federal government make a substantial investment in mass transit. In addition to being an essential service for low-income people, public transportation can improve the quality of life for millions of middle-class drivers who make increasingly long commutes from home to work, often in bumper-to-bumper traffic. Further, it promotes clean air and water, energy efficiency, economic efficiency, safety, and land conservation. Mass transit is not a local community issue; it is a national obligation. Yet federal transit funding dropped 30 percent between 1981 and 1988.[60] This policy must be reversed for the benefit of the environment and all of us.

Programs directed to meet the needs of occupants of public housing—the majority, women household heads and their families—are typically insufficient, misguided, and mismanaged by housing authorities. Therefore we must support the expansion of existing self-management programs for residents and demand that the federal government increase the supply of subsidized housing through rehabilitation and new construction. Less advantaged citizens have the right to live decently—without cockroaches, blocked toilets, and the humiliation of their poverty.

Because smaller paychecks may require women to share housing, we must create new lease agreements that recognize joint tenancy and co-liabilities among renters. We must eliminate single-family zoning which makes it illegal for people to live together unless they are related by blood, marriage, or adoption, and pass legislation prohibiting housing discrimination against lesbians and gay men. A household should be inclusively defined as an economic, social, and/ or sexual relationship of choice. This would put an end to absurd "moralistic" control over "legal" living arrangements, and would enable widows and divorced mothers living in no longer affordable large suburban houses to convert a portion of their homes into rental properties, and they should be receiving government grants to do so. Affordable rental housing is needed in America's suburbs, and American women who are homeowners badly need the income subsidy (see chapter 5).

Low-cost transitional housing for women going through a separation or divorce should be available in every community. Short-term residency should be an option for those who need or want it. Integrated support programs such as job counseling, legal services, health care, and childcare should be open to all. Large single-family houses, small apartment buildings, and hotels and motels could easily be converted for such purposes.

Other groups of women in our society have housing needs for which there are few or no assistance programs or people to advocate for them. These groups include nonresident domestic workers, Native American women who migrate to cities, women who leave mental institutions and prisons, teenage mothers, runaway teenagers, and women between the ages of fifty-five and sixty-five who are out of the work force and existing on marginal salaries but not yet eligible for retirement or senior citizen benefits. Another group, composed of disabled women, reports that placement in barrier-free housing and rehabilitation services favors men.[61] Further, housing units that are available to the women are frequently too small. Disabled women are not usually thought of as wives and mothers who often manage households with children and husbands. The wheelchair-accessible two- and three-bedroom unit is a rarity. The federal government must expand the funding for appropriately designed housing for the physically challenged. In the future, all housing must be routinely designed for wheelchair accessibility. In the next decades, mobility impairments will be commonplace, as the elderly population quadruples (see chapter 5). Further, when buildings include ramps as well as stairs, persons temporarily on crutches, and those with baby carriages, shopping carts, and bicycles benefit along with those disabled by birth, accident, illness, or aging.

Services traditionally carried out by a full-time homemaker must be provided as an integral part of housing. Domestic support services, so essential to single mothers, must also be available to dual-career couples living in conventional housing and to anyone else who wants and needs them. Federally funded neighborhood service houses could provide supervision of children's play and homework, visits to sick children, access to repair and delivery people, and hot meals for families to take home.

It is an absolute necessity of modern life that our housing be attached to a network of community-based social and domestic services. Only those with an investment in maintaining restrictive gender and class roles, and the human inequality they perpetuate, would deny this. But those who do should note that social as well as individual responsibility for the quality of domestic life harms no one and benefits everyone, including men, who are increasingly single parents, single people, and the husbands of working mothers.

Finally, women have traditionally achieved homeownership through marriage, divorce, widowhood, or inheritance. We need to develop alternate means through which more women can afford to become and remain homeowners, by creating nonprofit and cooperative housing; providing grants and self-sufficiency training for home maintenance, repairs, and weatherization; and legislating relief from escalating property taxes and fuel bills.[62] As long as homeownership is linked with status, power, and control, women have to be able to own their own homes—whether we agree with the ultimate wisdom of this system of enfranchisement or not.

The very nature of dignity requires each of us to have a place of our own where we can rest and renew ourselves. Women have not often or easily found such places. Their lower incomes, greater poverty and dependence on social assistance, responsibility for childbearing, and inferior and dependent social status have collectively contributed to the housing inequities they live with every day simply because they are women. The politics of housing has a profoundly detrimental impact on the quality of women's lives. We must not permit homes to be places of personal subordination. Susan B. Anthony wrote in 1877: "In woman's transition from the position of subject to sovereign, there must needs be an era of self-sustained, self-supported homes, where her freedom and equality shall be unquestioned."[63]

A direct, radical assault on the gender-based division of labor between the public, market economy and the private household is the only program through which women will alter their traditional economic and domestic positions. Any feminist proposal for housing must be a holistic one whose goal is not equality for women in the existing work force, but utter transformation of work and family life.

NOTES

1. For a fascinating history of the life and work of Catharine Beecher, see Kathryn Kish Sklar, *Catharine Beecher, A Study in American Domesticity* (New York: W. W. Norton, 1976).

2. Catharine Beecher and Harriet Beecher Stowe, *American Women's Home* (Hartford: Stowe-Day Foundation, 1975), 19.

3. Catharine Beecher, *A Treatise on Domestic Economy* (New York: Schocken, 1977), 2.

4. Beecher, *American Woman's Home,* 61.

5. Ibid., 13.

6. Dolores Hayden, "Catharine Beecher and the Politics of Housework," in *Women in American Architecture,* ed. Torre, 42.

7. Ruth Schwartz Cowan, "The 'Industrial Revolution' in the Home: Household Technology and Social Change in the 20th Century," *Technology and Culture* 17, no. 1 (January 1976): 10.

8. Robert C. Twombly, "Saving the Family: Middle-Class Attraction to Wright's Prairie House, 1901–1909," *American Quarterly* 27 (March 1975): 68.

9. Emily Post, *The Personality of a House* (New York: Funk and Wagnalls, 1948).

10. Ibid., 403.

11. Ibid., 196–97, 188.

12. Ibid., 3.

13. Ibid., 410.

14. Ibid., 320, 321.

15. Ibid., 7.

16. Ibid., 116.

17. Ibid., 165.

18. Ibid., 490–91.

19. Dorothy Field, *The Human House* (Boston: Houghton Mifflin, 1939), 11, as quoted in Gwendolyn Wright, "The Model Domestic Environment: Icon or Option," in *Women in American Architecture,* ed. Torre, 25.

20. Cowan, "Industrial Revolution," 13–15.

21. Ibid., 15.

22. Altman and Chemers, *Culture and Environment,* 192.

23. Lisa Belkin, "Bars to Equality of Sexes Seen as Eroding Slowly," *New York Times,* 20 August 1989, 1; and Arlie Hochschild, *The Second Shift* (New York: Viking, 1989), as quoted in Jim Miller, "Women's Work Is Never Done," *Newsweek,* 31 July 1989, 65.

24. Throughout the 1980s the FBI stated that wife abuse occurred every eighteen seconds. In a special NBC television news report, "Battered Women" (8 January 1990), the FBI statistic quoted was every fifteen seconds. Also see Minna Elias, "Man's Castle, Woman's Dungeon: Violence in the Home," *Seventh Sister* (March 1980), 3, and literature published by National Institute of Mental Health and the Family Violence Project of San Francisco.

25. Del Martin, *Battered Wives* (New York: Pocket Books, 1976), 13.

26. Ibid., 22.

27. Ibid., 15.

28. Lisa DiCaprio, "Women United for a Better Chicago," *New Women's Times* (June 1984): 10; Midgley, *Women's Budget*, 34.

29. Julia Robinson, Warner Shippee, Jennifer Schlemgin, and Razel Solow, *Women's Advocate's Shelter: An Evaluation* (St. Paul: University of Minnesota Center for Urban and Regional Affairs and School of Architecture and Landscape Architecture, 1982); and Lisbeth Wolf, director of the Women's Advocate's Shelter, St. Paul, Minnesota, phone interview with Leslie Kanes Weisman, 18 August 1989.

30. Robinson et al., *Women's Advocate's Shelter*, 71.

31. Monica Ehrler, "Additional Comments by Monica Ehrler" (July 1983), appendix to Robinson et al., *Women's Advocate's Shelter*, 72.

32. Ibid., 70; and Wolf, interview, 1989.

33. Martin, *Battered Wives*, 197.

34. Jo Freeman, "Women and Urban Policy," *Signs*, special issue, "Women and the City," supplement, vol. 5, no. 3 (Spring 1980): 11; and Canadian Council on Social Development, *Women in Need: A Sourcebook* (Ottawa: Canadian Council on Social Development, 1976), 69–82.

35. *A Statistical Portrait of Women in the United States* 23 (Washington, D.C.: U.S. Government Printing Office, 1978), and *Characteristics of the Population Below the Poverty Level* P-69, no. 124 (Washington, D.C.: U.S. Government Printing Office, 1978), 60. An excellent anthology on women, poverty, and housing is *The Unsheltered Woman: Women and Housing in the 1980s,* ed. Eugenie Ladner Birch (New Brunswick, N.J.: Center for Urban Policy Research, Rutgers University, 1985).

36. Freeman, "Women and Urban Policy," 14–15.

37. Department of Housing and Urban Development, Office of Public Policy and Research, *How Well Are We Housed? Female-Headed Households* (Washington, D.C.: U.S. Government Printing Office, 1978), 11–14.

38. Canadian Council on Social Development, *Women in Need*, 78.

39. Gerda R. Wekerle, "Women in the Urban Environment," *Signs*, special issue, "Women and the City," supplement, vol. 5, no. 3 (Spring 1980): 210.

40. Anne Gorman and Wendy Sarkissian, *No Room to Spare: Public Housing Options for Low-Income Single Persons* (Sydney: Housing Commission of New South Wales, 1982).

41. National Low Income Housing Coalition, "Triple Jeopardy: A Report on Low-Income Women and Their Housing Problems," unpublished paper, October 1980, 6; and Center on Budget and Policy Priorities, "A Place to Call Home: The Crisis in Housing for the Poor," unpublished paper, 1989, 1, 11.

42. Gwendolyn Wright, *Building the Dream: A Social History of Housing in America* (New York: Pantheon Books, 1981), 231.

43. Ibid., 220.

44. Ibid., 227.

45. Ibid., 221.

46. Roger Montgomery, "High Density, Low-Rise Housing and Changes in the American Housing Economy," in *The Form of Housing*, ed. Sam Davis (New York: Van Nostrand Reinhold, 1977), 105, 106.

47. Ibid., 107.

48. Wright, *Building the Dream*, 237.

49. Ibid.

50. Canadian Council on Social Development, *Women in Need*, 79.

51. Kimi Gray, "Meeting Our Housing Needs" (Speech delivered at "Sheltering Ourselves: Developing Housing for Women, A National Conference to Improve Housing for Women and Children," University of Cincinnati, 23 August 1987); and David Caprara, "Self-Help and Volunteerism: New Trends in Community Renewal," *CAUSA, USA Report* (October 1986): 1, 11.

52. Bertha Gilke, as interviewed by Gerda R. Wekerle, "Women as Urban Developers," *Women and Environments* 5, no. 2 (Summer 1982): 13–16.

53. Ibid., 16.

54. Art Levine with Dan Collins, "When Tenants Take Over, Public Housing Projects Get a New Lease on Life," *U.S. News and World Report*, 4 August 1986, 53, 54.

55. U.S. Department of Housing and Urban Development, "Nashville Public Housing Residents Buy Cooperative," *Recent Research Results* (December 1989): 1.

56. In 1980, 53 percent of American women heading households lived in apartments, compared to 35 percent of the general public. In a 1975 housing study, the National Council of Negro Women found that in American cities, 75 percent of female-headed households were renters. In Canada in 1977, 68.4 percent of renters were women. Further, women heading households in 1980 were three times more likely than others to experience involuntary displacement from their housing. In terms of income, regardless of occupation, women earn about 60 percent of the median earning of a comparable group of men. The average female college graduate earns less than the average white, male, high school dropout; and women have to work nine days to earn what men earn in five. While income varies substantially according to gender, a rent payment does not. Proportionately, all women must spend more of their income on housing, be it rented or owned, than men do. For more information see: National Low-Income Housing Coalition, "Triple Jeopardy," 2; National Council of Negro Women, *Women and Housing: A Report on Sex Discrimination in Five American Cities*, Commissioned by the U.S. Department of Housing and Urban Development, Office of the Assistant Secretary for Fair Housing and Equal Opportunity (Washington, D.C.: U.S. Government Printing Office, June 1975), 33; Janet McClain, "Access, Security, and Power: Women Are Still Second-Class Citizens in the Housing Market," *Status of Women News* 6, no. 1 (Winter 1979–80): 15; and *A Statistical Portrait of Women in the United States: 1978.*

57. In 1980, 26 percent of all rental units in America banned households with children; in Los Angeles, 70 percent of all advertised rental housing ex-

cluded or restricted children; in Dallas, 52 percent of existing apartment buildings were for adults only; in Atlanta, almost 75 percent of all new construction was restricted to adults. Other restrictions based on the number, age, or sex of children applied to about 55 percent of all rental units with two or more bedrooms in buildings that accepted children. One woman was reportedly told that two-bedroom apartments would be rented to female, single parents with one male child, but only one-bedroom apartments to those with one female child; in the latter case, parent and child would share the room regardless of age. Here the assumption is that a mother and daughter do not warrant or require mutual privacy, but sexual taboos and the higher status of a male child will insure privacy for a mother and her son. Marian Wright Edelman, *Portrait of Inequality: Black and White Children in America* (Washington D.C.: Children's Defense Fund, 1980), 40; and National Council of Negro Women, *Women and Housing*, 38.

58. Children's Defense Fund, "Families with Children Denied Housing," *CDF Reports* 2, no. 1 (March 1980): 4, 8; and Edelman, *Portrait of Inequality*, 46.

59. In 1985, the city of San Francisco adopted such an ordinance thanks to the efforts of City Supervisor Nancy Walker; "News from All Over," *Ms.*, March 1986, 25.

60. Midgley, *Women's Budget*, 27.

61. McClain, "Access, Security, and Power," 16.

62. Many low-income families spend more than 25 percent of their income on home energy and in cold-weather states it is not unusual for monthly energy bills to exceed total monthly income during the winter. In 1980, the Federal Low-Income Energy Assistance Program was established as part of the Oil Windfall Profits Tax to help low-income households offset huge increases in energy costs. The law gives priority to the aged and handicapped. Almost one-third of the 3.5 million households receiving assistance are composed of elderly women who face devastating choices of whether to eat, pay rent, or heat their homes. In 1989 the program was seriously underfunded and reached only a fraction of the thirteen million households eligible to participate. Midgley, *Women's Budget*, 14.

63. Susan B. Anthony, "Homes of Single Women" (October 1877), reprinted in *Ms.*, July 1979, 58.

5

Redesigning the Domestic Landscape

But you say . . . "a woman should give her whole life to the home." No, she should not. No human being should. She should serve society as does her human mate, and they, together, should go home to rest.

—Charlotte Perkins Gilman, 1904

Linking women's sexual and economic independence with new housing arrangements is not a recent idea. Feminists have continuously proclaimed that the traditional male-headed family and the single-family dream house are both oppressive and obsolete. Throughout the nineteenth and twentieth centuries, women promulgated proposals for liberating themselves from the tyranny of gender roles through redesigning the domestic environment and their relationship to it. For example, in 1868 a Cambridge, Massachusetts, housewife, Melusina Fay Pierce, organized women into producers' and consumers' cooperatives to perform domestic work collectively and charge their husbands retail prices equivalent to men's wages. In 1898 Charlotte Perkins Gilman, grandniece of Catharine Beecher and Harriet Beecher Stowe, published *Women and Economics,* in which she argued that human evolution was being retarded by women's confinement to housework. She supported a residence hotel of kitchenless apartments for working women, with linen service, childcare, and public dining. In 1916 Alice Constance Austin, a self-taught architect, presented her visionary model of a feminist socialist city for ten thousand people to be built in California. Houses were kitchenless, furniture was built in, beds rolled away, heated tile floors eliminated carpeting, and hot meals were delivered through underground tunnels from a central kitchen.[1]

Some of the architects of these schemes were viewed as heretics, advocates of "free love," socialists, and communists. Some of them were. Others were devout capitalists who believed in private property and the private house. All demanded the elimination of unpaid domestic work and women's confinement to it. They argued that the physical separation of domestic space from public space and the economic separation of the domestic economy from the political economy—both the results of industrial capitalism—had to be overcome if women were to be fully emancipated.

Their proposals were not perfect. Domestic work was still women's work for the most part, paid and professionalized though it was. The socioeconomic caste system remained, although there was usually an awareness of its injustice and of the schism it caused among women. Yet despite the efforts of these architects and thinkers, virtually all of our homes and communities have been designed, built, financed, and enforced by law to support the male-headed family. Housing design and policies are based upon the specious argument that all women will inevitably marry, have children, and spend most of their lives as non-wage-earning homemakers in shelter their husbands will pay for. But this assumption is wrong. Later marriage, smaller families, rising divorce and remarriage rates, longer life spans, and changing economic conditions have all driven women out of the home and into the paid work force.[2] The housing and neighborhoods we live in today are failing to meet the needs of the majority of American women and their families, for whom they were never intended.

How might we address the current misfit between old houses and new households? First, we will have to rid ourselves of both the female homemaker stereotype and our idea of the "typical" family. This will not be easy. The dispelling of the "family mystique" will be even more threatening to some than the discovery of the feminine mystique nearly three decades ago. Nonetheless, as long as society persists in ordaining the patriarchal family as a holy institution and as "morally superior," we will never design and build housing to enhance the lives of those who live differently, even if they are the majority.

Second, our housing will have to become spatially flexible, changeable over time according to household size and composition. Spatial variety is essential for supporting household diversity. If people cannot adapt their living space to suit their needs, they will adapt their needs to suit their living space, even if it is detrimental to their own well-being and to those with whom they live. We will have to find ways to accomplish this both through new housing and through the rehabilitation of our existing single-family housing. These houses, designed and built in an era characterized by energy affluence and one-paycheck families, are no longer affordable by the vast majority of American households, and there are few employed women or men today who are able to devote the amount of time required to manage and maintain them properly without assistance.

Most of these houses were built to extremely inefficient energy standards. The widespread use of large "picture windows" creates patterns of heat loss and gain that have to be compensated for by excessive heating or air conditioning. Typically, the houses are poorly insulated and improperly sited in blatant disregard of sun orientation, a site-planning strategy designed to maximize builders' profits. Nevertheless, the owner-occupied single-family house is our most numerous and desirable housing type; in 1980 there were over fifty million of them in American suburbs, constituting two-thirds of our nation's total housing units.[3] In the near future many people, especially households with children, are going to want or have to live in these houses for some time to come; and we are going to have to find ways of adapting these buildings to more realistic energy standards for households of diverse sizes and incomes.

Finally, if women are to be freed from their primary responsibility as sole caretakers of the home, the local community, rather than the family, will have to take on some of the chores that traditionally tie women to the home. Current planning proposals for commercial, profit-making, neighborhood laundry and dry-cleaning establishments, fast-food restaurants, and childcare centers do not challenge conventional gender roles or the primacy of the private single-family house. They simply offer those families who can afford to pay for these costly services the opportunity to do so. They expand the consumer role of the nuclear family and amplify class privileges and penalties. In the long run, they are inimical to the meaning of feminism. If we are to transcend these conceptual limitations, it is crucial that we understand the redoutable role the conventional family has played in shaping our identities.

The Family Mystique

In 1978 there were about seventy-six million households in America; only 17 percent of them included a father as the sole wage earner, a mother who was a full-time homemaker, and one or more children (and only 7 percent with two or more children); and over one-third of these women said they planned to look for work outside the home at some time in their lives. By 1980, one out of every four households was headed by women; and in 1982 nearly half of all couples with children had two-paycheck marriages. Increasingly, people are finding themselves, through choice or life circumstance, living as couples without children, living communally in shared housing with others to whom they are not related, or living alone. In 1980, 22 percent of American households consisted of single people; a third of these were women over sixty-five; and by the late 1980s singles headed 45 percent of all households.[4]

Yet, our patriarchal society has long done its very best to uphold the dominance of the sacred, male-headed family. Even quite recently, priests and politicians alike have conspired to keep the continuous existence of dual and female-headed families a secret, despite all facts to the contrary. For example, in 1979, the White House scheduled a Conference on Families which was abruptly cancelled. The problems began when some participating Catholic priests discovered that the conference coordinator, an eminent black woman, was divorced and raising her family as a single parent; and when they found out that only 7 percent of Americans lived in the type of "quintessential" household they so passionately celebrated, they decided to call the whole thing off.[5] Another example can be found in our census methods, which, until the late 1970s, assumed that every family had one head, always a husband. Therefore only those families without husbands could be female-headed.[6] In 1988, George Bush ran his successful presidential campaign on the promulgation of "traditional family values."

Women have always worked outside the home. Most of them have had to, especially poor and working-class women who, like men, work to support themselves and their families. Idealization of the patriarchal family as the norm, all others therefore being deviant, led one unemployed man during the Depression to lament, "I would rather turn on the gas and put an end to the whole family than let my wife support me."[7]

Women living without men pose an even greater threat to the maintenance of the "family mystique." Throughout history there have always been women who have lived alone or with each other. According to the sociologist Elise Boulding, in any period for which data are available, in any setting, urban or rural, one-fifth to one-half of the heads of households were women. The world figure in 1980 was 38 percent.[8]

Women who have chosen not to share their homes with men have done so at great personal risk. They have been stigmatized as "old maids," lesbians, "unfeminine," pitiable, and unfulfilled. During the four nightmarish centuries in which millions of women were tortured and murdered as witches, women who headed their own households were the most likely to be accused and condemned.[9]

During the Middle Ages, women living independently of men were routinely punished and persecuted. The courts not infrequently sentenced them to "hanging, being buried alive, or drowning by being placed in a cage and lowered into the river." Unpartnered women were forced into segregated housing. In 1493 one European city passed the following ordinance: "All married women living apart from their husbands and girls of evil life shall go to the brothels."[10]

It would not be difficult to find, in any historical era, examples of the relentless and often brutal social pressures applied to women in order to protect the primacy of the male-headed family, including the effort to portray female-headed families as pathologically deviant. However, one contemporary example will suffice. "The Negro Family: The Case for National Action" is the formal title of a document prepared by Harvard professor Daniel Patrick Moynihan for a presidential commission during the mid-sixties, at the height of the civil rights movement. The Moynihan report declared that the predominance of black women as family heads was responsible for all of the drug abuse, crime, and promiscuity that allegedly characterized the Negro family. His remedy was to introduce "patriarchal relations in the Black community, identical to those obtaining in the dominant culture."[11]

The Moynihan report was wrong in many respects. Even though families headed by women can be found more often in black than white families, at least 70 percent of black families are now and have consistently been headed jointly by a man and a woman. In some historical periods the percentages of black and white families headed by women have been identical.[12] But perhaps more important, as Bettina Aptheker cogently explains, the Moynihan report is an indictment of all women. "It is a warning to white women that if they persist in entering the workforce as their black sisters have done . . . they too will endanger the basic structural unit of society—the nuclear family under male provision. In this way, white women invite social chaos and economic ruin, and they too will pay the penalty of such a transgression."[13]

This vehement enforcement by our patriarchal society of the traditional "all-American family" makes it easy to understand why the majority probably still believes it to be the norm, and no doubt explains why many still aspire to live that way. But there are fewer who do and fewer still who will achieve it for any length of time. Although most people do marry, divorce rates have soared and few women spend their entire lives at home without a salaried job.

In recognition of these changing conditions of work and family life, in 1984 there was a national competition that called for imaginative design proposals for the "new American house," suitable for the "contemporary American family." The winning team—Jacqueline Leavitt, a planner, and Troy West, an architect—designed townhouses for active households of singles, related adults, and single parents with little time for housework and little need to do formal entertaining (see fig. 19). Each unit is just under a thousand square feet and contains a one-story office space along the street, connected by a linear kitchen-dining area and private garden courtyard to a three-level living space with two bedrooms and a shared bath. The lack of a designated master bedroom allows for more flexibility in the way the house is used. Two units can be "flipped" in plan to form a daycare center in the two offices, congregate housing for two single parents with up to four children, and one "granny flat." The main part of each house opens onto a common outdoor space.

Housing innovations like those of Leavitt and West are timely and increasingly essential. According to a study done by the MIT-Harvard Joint Center for Urban Studies, twenty million new American households were formed between 1980 and 1990. Only three million of them consisted of married couples with children at home. The rest consisted of a combination of single people, single-parent households that are mostly female-headed, couples without children, and aged persons.[14]

These are not just statistics. These are the people we know in our everyday lives. It is doubtful that the 93 percent of Americans who are currently living in "nontraditional" patterns think of themselves as "deviant." Families do not deviate, they simply differ. But this does not mean that American families are hopelessly collapsing, rather that people are living in more diverse ways to achieve the intimacy and support that constitutes a family—and we must affirm and support that diversity in housing design, policies, and practices.

Housing Preferences and Needs

Studies show that most Americans say they prefer to live in single-family houses, including those who live in apartments or other multi-family housing.[15] Certainly they do. The private house is sacred to Americans, an icon of status, security, stability, and family life. Our notion of "home" as a permanent, detached object is deeply rooted in our expectations and consciousness as a nation. We have been so

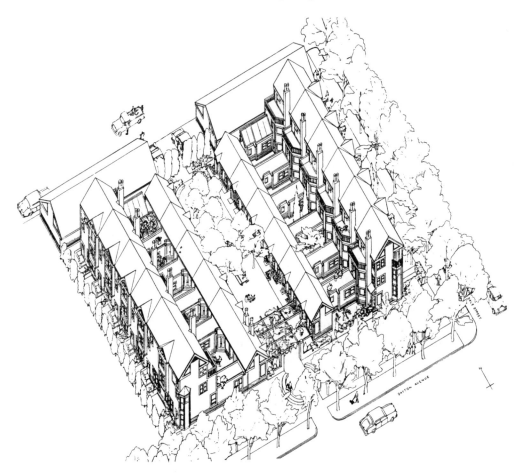

Figure 19. A New American House, Dayton Court, St. Paul, Minnesota, 1986, Troy West Associates, architect. This design is a modified version of the winning entry to a 1984 national competition for housing for the contemporary American family submitted by planner Jacqueline Leavitt and architect Troy West. Drawing courtesy Troy West, architect.

thoroughly socialized to accept this archetypal house that no other form of housing evokes the same warm connotations.

But attitudes can and do change. A century ago, debt was a terrible social taboo. By the turn of the century it was a virtual necessity for the would-be homeowner. Today, housing indebtedness is a well-established, perfectly respectable fact of life for Americans. Similarly, not very long ago, a young couple generally began married life in rented, multifamily housing, an apartment or "duplex." After three or four years of marriage and the birth of a child or two, they bought a Cape Cod or a small ranch "starter house." Today they are more likely to buy a condominium. The primary reason is economic; the secondary reason is social. A condominium costs less than a house in a comparable neighborhood, offers the financial advantages of home-ownership, may include recreational amenities such as tennis courts and swimming pools that residents could not otherwise afford, and is easier to maintain than a private house—an incentive for older people, dual-career couples, and working singles. It is estimated that by the year 2000 almost half of the American population will live in condominiums.[16] We can count on the fact that condominium living will appreciate in status accordingly.

Residential builders and developers are in business to make a profit; they will build whatever housing they are convinced will sell. Some have begun to experiment with shared housing directed toward middle-income singles, often professionals, who cannot afford to buy a house of their own. Townhouses, condominiums, and cooperative apartments designed specifically for singles to share are known as "mingles" housing, so called because the occupants are often unrelated friends or coworkers. Mingles units usually include two "master bedrooms" each with private bath, sometimes with private sitting areas. The living area, kitchen, and dining room are shared. Singles who opt for the mingles plan usually sign the mortgage together and split the down payment, monthly payments, and income tax benefits. Many of the "tandem" buyers of mingles housing are professional women, since they are likely to earn about 40 percent less than their male colleagues. Mingles housing in most respects is essentially like traditional single-family housing. What is different is the expectation of who will live there, what their relationships will be, and the recognition of their need for equality, autonomy, and privacy.[17]

Since there are so few alternatives to conventional housing at present, we really do not know what different households would actually choose if they had a real choice. People choose their housing based on what they can afford, in the neighborhood they prefer. The fact that increasing numbers of single men are buying suburban houses, according to real estate agents and sociologists, may reflect a preference for the suburbs, not the single-family house per se.[18]

We must be careful to avoid stereotypical generalizations when considering people's housing preferences and needs. Just as households vary, so do the people within them. For example, not all single parents are interested in novel housing arrangements that encourage cooperative or communal cooking, laundry, or childcare. Some middle- and upper-class working mothers might find enough benefits in such housing, having already lived in the conventional kind, that they would willingly give up their large, private dream kitchens. But many poor and working-class women are still waiting for the not-so-novel, decent housing that this country promised all Americans decades ago. Those waiting for the dream to be fulfilled may find it difficult, if not impossible, to give up what they have never had.

Similarly, despite the myth that all older people love children, apparently not all of them want to live with children as their neighbors. "No one loves children as much as I do," said one retired grandmother who lives in an adults-only complex in Maryland. "But it's quiet here. There are no toys to stumble over in the hallways, no whining or screaming."[19] On the other hand, there are also many older people who strongly advocate intergenerational living, who believe that retirement communities and senior citizen housing projects are socially unwholesome.

If we really want to create housing that will respond intelligently and sensitively to different human needs, we will first have to uncover and eliminate the policies that are operating in our society to preserve the privileged status of the male-headed family and the single-family house.

Residential Zoning and Social Conformity

Land use zoning is one of the major social policies preventing developers, architects, and others in the building industry from responding to the demand for innovative, nonconventional housing. Like the public buildings discussed in chapter 2, zoning enforces the social caste system by segregating "family" from "nonfamily" households, rich from poor, black from white. Zoning was originally developed to protect human health and welfare and the property values of homeowners by segregating land use (through separating commercial, industrial, and residential areas) and regulating population density through establishing the size of lots and the square footage of dwellings and other actions. Municipalities and the courts use zoning, however, as a mechanism to achieve social conformity.

The "single-family" zoning ordinance which regulates the physical form of virtually all of suburbia and much of urban America is especially iniquitous. Originally, the phrase "single family" was intended to describe a particular type of house, not a particular type of household. It was meant to distinguish the private house from apartments, boardinghouses, residence halls, hotels, and trailers. As used, the single-family ordinance prohibits all but persons related by blood, marriage, or adoption from residing in the area it covers.[20]

Historically, American courts have assiduously endorsed residential zoning regulations that protect the single-family house and its male-headed family. A 1925 California Supreme Court decision that upheld the zoned exclusion of multifamily dwellings is typical:

> The establishment of single family districts is for the general welfare because it tends to promote and perpetuate the American home.... The home and its intrinsic influences are the very foundation of good citizenship, and any factor contributing to the establishment of homes and the fostering of home life doubtless tends to the enhancement not only of community life but of the life of the nation as a whole.... It is needless to further analyze and enumerate all of the factors which make a single family home more desirable for the promotion and perpetuation of family life. It will suffice to say that there is a sentiment practically universal that this is so.[21]

A more recent ruling, *Palo Alto Tenants Union v. Morgan* (1970), which upheld the exclusion of a communal group, reveals how tenacious this reverence for the family is. The court stated: "The traditional family is an institution reinforced by biological and legal ties which are difficult or impossible to sunder.... It has been a means for countless millennia, of satisfying the deepest emotional and physical needs of human beings."[22]

Discriminatory community zoning and planning boards employ this single-family statute as a means of preserving what they call "neighborhood character," a euphemistic designation that excludes anyone whose lifestyle they do not condone, such as unmarried couples, gay couples, and those living communally. Single-family zoning is thus justified on "moral" grounds because nonconforming households allegedly endanger the traditional family and its values. Nancy Rubin, in her book *The New Suburban Woman*, writes about a lesbian couple who experienced so much harassment and public embarrassment that they finally decided to move. One of the women told her: "It's much safer and smarter to 'go underground' in the suburbs if you are a lesbian than to openly acknowledge it. In the city, people don't care so much about who you are or what your sexual preference might be. But in the suburb you are in trouble unless you can be very discreet. Suburban men and women get very upset because they feel that if you are a homosexual you represent a challenge to their life-style."[23]

The fear of "nontraditional" sexuality is one motive for enforcement of exclusionary zoning; excluding people with lower incomes from affluent neighborhoods is another. The establishment of a minimum square footage for dwellings and minimum lot sizes guarantees the construction of relatively large and relatively expensive single-family houses that moderate- and low-income families cannot afford. Further, it prevents the possibility of building low- and moderate-cost housing.

Zoning has also been used to ensure that the boundaries of the affluent white suburbs and the impoverished black and Hispanic ghettos that form America's urban pattern would be drawn with indelible colored lines on the patriarchal map of social injustice. Residential segregation was historically fostered as a desirable way of life by the Federal Housing Administration (FHA). Page after page of official FHA documents were written in the covert language of racism. For example, one technical bulletin from the mid-1940s advised developers to "concentrate on a particular market, based on age, income, and race." Wherever "Negro invasion" threatened "neighborhood homogeneity," the FHA refused to underwrite mortgages (called "redlining"). The private banks and savings and loan associations followed suit, causing stable working-class neighborhoods like Detroit's Lower East Side and North Philadelphia to deteriorate as rents rose and services shrank because houses could not be sold.[24]

In the suburbs, the FHA openly encouraged the use of restrictive zoning covenants, allegedly to "preserve neighborhood stability and character," but in reality to enforce segregation and prevent the decline in property values that characterized "changing" neighborhoods. The 1947 FHA manual stated: "If a mixture of user groups is found to exist, it must be determined whether the mixture will render the neighborhood less desirable to present and prospective occupants. Protective covenants are essential to the sound development of proposed residential areas since they regulate the use of land and provide a basis for the development of harmonious, attractive neighborhoods."[25] With such generous support from the federal government, builders, bankers, and businessmen could guarantee suburban homeowners that their neighbors would be of the same race, religion, ethnicity, and socioeconomic class.

Blacks were not silent or naive about these practices. The National Association for the Advancement of Colored People (NAACP) charged the FHA with "fostering black ghettos through urban redlining and suburban discrimination" but could do nothing to actually change it. In 1948 the Supreme Court outlawed restrictive covenants, but it took the FHA two years to announce officially that it would no longer issue mortgages in restricted neighborhoods. Further, FHA officials continued to approve "unwritten agreements and existing 'traditions' of segregation until 1968."[26]

But in the last two decades, faced with a national housing crisis, ongoing pressure from civil rights activists, and the extraordinary preponderance of "nontraditional" families, the courts have begun to challenge discriminatory traditions and to question the constitutionality of zoning practices that violate the equal protection doctrine.[27] Several court decisions have incorporated a statutory definition of "family" as a single housekeeping unit, thereby "conferring family status on a sorority, a group of novices and their Mother Superior, and even a college residence hall housing sixty."[28]

In 1970 the Illinois Supreme Court, in *City of Des Plaines v. Trottner*, supported the protection of associational rights of individuals, stating that zoning ordinances that "penetrate so deeply into the internal composition of a single housekeeping unit [are] overextensions of the police power."[29] In 1971, citing *Trottner*, the New Jersey Supreme Court "decisively rejected the single family blood relation criteria," in *Kirsch Holding Co. v. Borough of Manasquan*, stressing the "emerging right of unrelated people in reasonable numbers to have recourse to common housekeeping facilities."[30] The New Jersey Supreme Court's 1975 *Mount Laurel I* ruling stated that all developing municipalities must "affirmatively afford" equal housing opportunities by permitting apartments and multifamily homes that the poor could afford.[31]

The history of the Mount Laurel decision reveals the complex difficulties involved in reconciling the private interest of those who would maintain racial and economic segregation with the public obligation of the courts to ensure that all citizens are adequately housed. Late in the 1960s, most of Mount Laurel's black families lived in miserable conditions in the Springville area of the township's dusty east side. The first of several huge tract developments were just starting to be built a few miles away, and Mount Laurel's building inspectors had the old tarpaper shacks and converted chicken coops in Springville condemned and torn down, but not replaced.

Springville residents, fearing that the loss of low-cost housing might force them to move to the North Camden slums, formed the Springville Action Committee, spearheaded by Ethel Lawrence. When the township rejected the residents' plans to use federal funds to build a low-income housing project, they retained Camden Region Legal Services and, with the NAACP, filed the class-action suit against Mount Laurel that resulted in the New Jersey Supreme Court's 1975 ruling. By 1983 an avalanche of countersuits resulted in a second court decision known as *Mount Laurel II*. It reiterated the constitutional obligation set out in 1975 that all developing municipalities generate a "fair share" of their region's present and prospective low- and moderate-income housing, but provided a new "builder's remedy" to enforce the doctrine.

The courts would allow a developer to build more houses on the same piece of property than allowed by local zoning. Profits from the additional units would help lower the price of units set aside for sale to needy families. The usual ratio was four market-rate condominiums or townhouses for every moderately priced dwelling. Thus, if the court found a municipality responsible for providing a thousand low-cost units, invoking the builder's remedy could force the community to accept five thousand new houses. Since some suburban communities were assigned fair-share numbers by the court that would have doubled their housing stock, local politicians, afraid that hordes of poor people from the cities would invade their neighborhoods, vowed to go to jail rather than follow the court's orders.

After months of legal wrangling, the Fair Housing Act of 1985 was amended to the legislation as a compromise to help it pass. This act established the Council on Affordable Housing, composed of private citizens, builders, and public officials, to settle zoning disputes in municipalities that had been brought to court. In addition, it established a mechanism called regional contribution agreements (RCA's), which allowed suburbs to transfer up to half of the housing units they were ordered to build, along with sufficient funds to build them, to willing cities within their region. Still, the legal battles did not end. The law and its provisions were challenged until, finally, in February 1986, the Supreme Court issued another decision, now referred to as *Mount Laurel III*, which upheld the Fair Housing Act.

The Council on Affordable Housing that replaced the court as judge in Mourt Laurel disputes has been far less assertive in its requirements of municipalities. Once established, the council immediately recalculated the state's affordable housing need and reduced it from the 277,808 units reached by the court to 145,707. It allowed municipalities to lower their quotas further by crediting them for subsidized apartments built since 1980, for accessory apartments built in the basements and garages of existing single-family houses, and for environmentally sensitive land considered unbuildable. It also offered municipalities protection from builder's remedy suits by developers if they submitted plans for providing moderately priced housing. By May 1988, 134 communities had done so, 42 towns had been exempted, and 71 communities had obligations of fewer than 10 low-cost units. However, some communities have responded with a shower of ideas for meeting their fair-share obligation, including establishing nonprofit development corporations and housing authorities.[32]

Although Mount Laurel legislation has resulted in an increase in low-income housing in New Jersey, RCA's that allow prosperous suburban communities to avoid their responsibility to build low-income housing by transfering money to poorer urban communities run counter to the Supreme Court's clear intent to encourage enconomic and racial integration in the suburbs. More than two decades after Ethel Lawrence and others began their struggle, the poor are still being pushed out of Mount Laurel by the rich, who can afford to pay to keep them excluded. Nevertheless, the Mount Laurel ruling is of major importance. Several states, including California and New Hampshire, have cited it in dealing with their own housing and zoning problems; and in March 1988 a federal appeals court struck down a Huntington, Long Island, zoning ordinance, not because it did not allow affordable, multifamily housing, but because it allowed such residences to be built only in areas already occupied predominantly by minorities.[33]

Favorable court decisions like *Mount Laurel* and those previously cited have made important contributions to a growing argument for flexibility and reform of elitist single-family zoning—clearing the way for economically, socially, and racially diverse households and the construction of mixed and innovative housing that will support their different needs and lifestyles. But these reforms are hardly ubiquitous and they are not enough.

Communities must give architects, planners, and developers the opportunity to preserve open land, inhibit suburban sprawl, and provide affordable housing by allowing cluster zoning where private houses are sited closer together in order to leave large parcels of shared open land intact; compact lot zoning that permits smaller houses to be built on smaller lots; and zero lot line zoning that shifts the siting of a house to the edge of the lot on one side to gain a larger, usable side yard.

Further, zoning that segregates the use of land must also be jettisoned. Currently, residential zoning excludes home occupations that could make the combination of work and family responsibilities infinitely easier for many women and men. It also prohibits services essential to women and their families, such as childcare, daycare for the elderly, and shelters for battered women. Finally, conventional zoning permits the planning of low-density residential neighborhoods without local stores and local jobs, which, while possibly suitable for small children, often breeds boredom and a sense of isolation in teenagers, adults, and the older population.[34]

Not all American suburbs are antisocial. Radburn, in Fairlawn, New Jersey, was designed in 1929 by Henry Wright and Clarence Stein as a comprehensively planned community that would foster neighborly involvement and protect children from the dangers of the increasingly omnipresent automobile. At Radburn, nicknamed "The Town for the Motor Age," the car was accepted as inevitable but was not allowed to dominate the environment. Pedestrians and vehicular traffic were separated by doing away with the traditional gridiron street pattern and replacing it with the superblock, a large area of land surrounded by main roads. Houses are grouped around small cul-de-sacs connected to the main roads by small access streets. Land inside the superblock consists of lush green parks, gardens, and footpaths. The living and sleeping rooms of the houses face the park; service rooms such as kitchens and baths face the access streets. Children can play in safety in the parks and walk to the community school without ever crossing a vehicular road. The housing itself is diverse in size, cost, and type and includes single-family houses, townhouses, duplexes, and apartments. The Radburn Association employs a paid staff and recreation director to maintain the twenty-three-acre parks network, buildings and grounds, recreation amenities, and community center with offices, library, kitchen, community room, and playhouse, and to provide a "well-integrated recreational and social program at all age levels." All residents pay mandatory association dues.[35]

Today Radburn continues to flourish as a desirable and vital community. Like most of suburbia, it too is "greying"; there are far fewer children and many more older residents. The variety in housing size and type now supports a variety of household sizes, incomes, and lifestyles—from two-paycheck couples of the opposite or same sex who commute to work on the nearby train, to single people who work at home.[36]

For over fifty years Radburn has been an inspiration to architects, planners, and those who live there. There are important lessons to be learned from the "Radburn idea." The social, architectural, and planning principles employed by Wright and Stein can be used to reorganize spatially the typical "antisocial" suburban neighborhood of today. For example, the architect Dolores Hayden suggests that individual backyards be joined together to form public commons and gardens; side yards and front lawns become fenced, private spaces; and private garages be converted to public garages, laundries, daycare facilities, community centers, kitchens, and rental apartments.[37] Clearly, if enough resources and talent are available it is possible to design and build housing in attractive, healthy communities that enhance the human spirit. However, if we are to do so for both the privileged and those of less exalted circumstances, we will have to change not only the nature of the restrictive zoning covenants that stand in our way but also the social attitudes that created them.

Transforming the Single-Family House

Millions of American families already regularly ignore proscriptive zoning regulations by subdividing single-family houses into illegal two- and three-family dwellings through converting a basement, attic, garage, or spare bedroom or two into a small rental unit called an accessory apartment.

The Bureau of the Census estimates that between 1970 and 1980 there were as many as 2.5 million units created nationwide.[38] In 1983 New York City's Commissioner of Housing Preservation and Development likened the generally widespread acceptance of this illegality to the situation during Prohibition.[39] By 1989 the practice was so commonplace that some communities, such as the San Francisco suburb of Daly City; Boulder, Colorado; Montgomery County, Maryland; Weston, Connecticut; and Babylon, Long Island, had legalized accessory apartments so that they could be regulated according to safe housing standards. But these are exceptions. Other communities have hired more building inspectors to find illegal apartments and evict tenants. Most communities are avoiding facing the issue by simply looking the other way.

When an accessory apartment is added, the house usually remains owner-occupied and there is little or no change in the exterior, so that it still looks like a single-family dwelling. Often a separate entry/exit to the outside is created, or an existing stair, landing, and door are appropriated to ensure privacy for resident owner and the tenants of the new apartment.

The primary motive in creating separate quarters for a renter, grown children, or aging parents in single-family houses is economic. In 1981, American housing experts estimated that only 5 percent of the nation's families could afford to buy a new house since the average cost required an annual income of about $60,000—a figure well above the median household income.[40] Today, as the median house price continues to rise much faster than the median income, homeownership virtually requires two paychecks per household and is still beyond the reach of the majority of potential buyers. The National Association of Home Builders (NAHB) estimates that between 1989 and 1993, some 59 million Americans will pass through the twenty-five-to-thirty-four age category (the traditional age for first-time home buyers). Less than half of them will be able to buy homes during that time.[41]

As a result, many homeowners are locked into their houses, unable to sell advantageously in today's market and unable to maintain them on their own. Many of these homeowners are suburban women who have "aged in place." Their children have grown and moved away; their husbands are gone; their mortgages were paid off long ago. Now they have more space than they need, and soaring fuel bills, taxes, and maintenance costs make their houses increasingly difficult to afford. Renting out an accessory apartment gives them the additional income they require to stay in their homes. At the same time, it is a very cost-effective means of increasing the critically low supply of affordable rental units in the suburbs, thereby allowing lower-income people to live in neighborhoods they could not normally afford.

In 1983 it cost about $10,000 to create an accessory apartment compared to a cost of $40,000 to $60,000 for an equivalent new unit.[42] The building industry is likely to support these conversions. During the same year only 1.5 percent of American housing stock was new construction. Rehabilitating the remaining 98.5 percent, valued at $1.5 trillion, is a viable way for builders to provide affordable housing, thereby staying in business.[43] Further, communities facing the depletion or destruction of valuable wetlands, woods, farmland, or shorelines by the construction of new housing developments should endorse accessory apartments as an environmentally sound means of providing financially accessible housing that also adds to municipal income through increased property taxes.

Those who argue against adding accessory apartments to single-family houses say they change the character of the neighborhood, lower property values, and cause traffic congestion and pressure on community services ranging from fire protection and sewage treatment to mass transit. The veracity of these arguments varies significantly among different communities, and depends in part on whether or not such units are legally regulated. Further, the inclusion of an accessory apartment unit within a single-family house does not necessarily mean that more people will be living in the house than the numbers for which it was originally designed—only that the occupants will be living there in greater privacy. Certainly, racial and socioeconomic prejudice is an important element of civic opposition.

In any case, the proliferation and legalization of accessory apartments is inevitable as a stop-gap solution to the much larger problem of providing affordable housing, since the next best thing to reducing the price of a house or providing mortgage subsidies is a greater utilization of existing dwellings. For the first time, the impetus for reform of single-family zoning and housing is coming from local residents themselves, not from outsiders to the community. Motivated by financial need, they represent a strong political constituency that could turn our housing crisis into a housing opportunity that will significantly benefit today's "nontraditional" households.

The economic advantages of accessory housing accrue especially to older homeowners (most often widows living on fixed incomes), to renters, singles, and lower-income families, since rents are usually lower than for a conventional apartment. Women are a majority in all of these groups. There are also important social benefits inherent in this domestic arrangement. Planning consultant Patrick Hare explains: "When we talk about releasing housing by breaking down existing single family zoning . . . we're talking about releasing human resources, because single family zoning by definition almost precludes exchange of services between households. They're too far apart. . . . We are talking about retrofitting suburban family development to permit extended family living or surrogate extended family living."[44]

This housing concept is especially important to divorced women, particularly divorced mothers. The rent from an accessory apartment may enable these women, who might otherwise have to give up their houses, to hold onto them. A 1985 California study of three thousand divorcing couples reported that in the first year after divorce, wives' incomes dropped 73 percent while husbands' increased by 42 percent.[45] Women who remain in their family houses after a divorce sooner or later have to face the fact that they are "house poor." Unable to keep up with yard care, peeling paint, leaks in the roof, and rising fuel bills without their husbands' income, eventually most of them are forced to move. And when they do, most of them end up moving into inferior housing in a lower-status neighborhood where they feel they do not belong. This is true regardless of race or socioeconomic class.[46]

All people have ideas about what is appropriate housing for their families or lifestyles. Feelings of well-being or deprivation are closely attached to living in a dwelling and neighborhood that is compatible with one's self-image. Women who are unable to maintain continuity in their housing after a divorce suffer a painful loss of self-esteem at a time when they are especially vulnerable. Similarly, there is a much higher incidence of deterioration among aged people when they are removed from the security of a familiar environment. The accessory apartment offers an excellent solution to displacement and downward mobility.

Ironically, yet another group that would benefit from this transformation of the single-family house is the traditional nuclear family. In the United States in 1983, 19.1 million people over the age of eighteen and 4.5 million over twenty-five lived with their parents.[47] They are mostly young adults who cannot find jobs or afford their own apartments in today's economy. Increasingly unable to make it on their own, young married couples and those who divorce "come home." While this may solve some financial problems for parents and their rent-paying offspring, it frequently creates emotional problems for all. Mothers no longer want the responsibility of "family-sized" meals and loads of laundry. Grown children usually want their privacy and independence too. Separate but attached living quarters could unquestionably mitigate family tensions. Further, the rental income generated from an accessory apartment could enable a young couple to meet the mortgage payments on a suburban house they could not otherwise afford.

A spatially different but conceptually similar version of the accessory apartment has been available in Australia for many years. Called "Granny flats," "elder cottages," or "echo housing," these accommodations are completely independent additions to the side or rear yard of a detached house. In this arrangement, an older person or couple lives in a small, low-cost, prefabricated house, comparable to a "trailer home," installed in their grown child's backyard. The older person continues to live independently with help and companionship nearby. In Australia the government rents out the movable cottages. When the parent moves or dies, the cottage is returned and set up in someone else's backyard. In the United States, private corporations could build, lease, or sell echo houses to homeowners for use by various household members at different life-stages—from teenagers to newlyweds to retirees.

This housing concept of privacy with proximity among household members has important implications for maintaining the quality of family life, be they nuclear families or families of choice. In the former case, studies show that older people feel that moving in with an adult child is the least desirable way to live. Most of those who do are mothers living in their daughters' homes, since daughters are expected to maintain kinship ties and provide a home for an ailing or widowed parent.[48] The fear of role reversal from autonomy to dependency haunts many an aging parent and angers and confuses many a loving child. In the latter case, such housing arrangements could support and sustain intergenerational and/or intimate friendships and relationships among singles and couples of the same or opposite sex.

It is a scandalous tragedy that 40 percent of elderly Americans in nursing homes are not sick; they simply have no place else to go. So they are forced to live at worst with "filthy corridors, abusive orderlies, and miserable food," and at best with "isolation from society, loneliness, and feelings of uselessness," according to the Gray Panthers, an advocacy group for the rights of older citizens.[49]

Of course these housing problems affect elderly women and men alike; it is simply that the aging population is increasingly female. In 1982, 59 percent of those over sixty-five were women, and at the oldest level, women outnumbered men two to one.[50] While the vast majority of men over sixty-five were still married, most women over sixty-five (75 percent) were widows, and over half of them lived alone. They are among the most poverty stricken of all people, especially if they are Hispanic or Asian-Americans. They have the smallest incomes, the smallest budget for housing and related services, live in the worst housing conditions, and have the most health problems.[51]

In the near future, the elderly will constitute the largest special-needs population in terms of housing. As the eighty-five-and-older population quadruples in the United States in the next forty years, we will have no place to put them. We would need to add 220 new nursing-home beds every day between 1989 and the year 2000 just to meet the demands of the 1990s; and the already high annual costs of $23,000 to $60,000 per person for nursing-home care will soar as demand exceeds supply.[52]

By the year 2010, the baby-boom generation will begin turning sixty-four. By 2025, the Census Bureau estimates that for every 100 middle-aged persons there will be 253 senior citizens. By 2030, all of the baby-boomers—77 million people, one-third of the current United States population—will be senior citizens.[53] Perhaps no change in the twenty-first century will have a more profound effect on how American society will look, feel, think, and behave. Families will feel the strains of the aging society acutely. Not only will the percentage of elderly be greater, but people will be old much longer. Four-generation families will be the norm, and many will have to choose between sending a child to college or grandma to a nursing home. The baby boomers who remained childless will find themselves particularly strapped for care and housing in old age.

Increasingly, seniors will be living at subsistence levels. Today's deteriorating homeownership rates will have a ripple effect across the years. Traditionally the American home has been the most important vehicle for savings that the United States has to offer, a house rising in value and equity as the mortgage is paid. Many of today's priced-out younger couples and singles may never be able to buy—with worrisome consequences for their later lives—since they will probably not have the same wealth base to draw on in retirement as today's retirees who are homeowners. This affordability gap could be the first step toward creating a new class of elderly who, without an equity cushion to cash in on after retiring, would have to depend even more heavily on a social security system whose future already looks shaky.

In addition to living with grown children, in retirement communities, and in nursing homes, the elderly will increasingly band together in dormitories, shared apartments, boardinghouses, single room occupancy hotels, and communes to save money, find companionship, and reduce their sense of isolation. Life-care cooperative housing that provides independent living with a gradient of domestic and health-care services made available as they are needed will become the norm. To date the small numbers of life-care cooperative communities that have been built are available only to the very affluent, usually those who have a house to sell to raise the hundreds of thousands of dollars required to buy in. In the next decade, life-care housing must be designed, managed, and made affordable for all who will want it.

Older people differ and so does their housing. Some own estates, stocks, and precious possessions. Others can carry their possessions in a shopping bag. But to a greater or lesser degree, all of them will face the insidious loss of social function and status that accompanies aging in our society. One important determining factor will be the circumstances in which they are housed. Regardless of income, race, or gender, all older people must have access to secure, socially supportive housing that empowers them with the dignity of independence.

Housing that Works for Single Parents

Independence for millions of women who are low-income single mothers is also linked to housing designed to promote self-sufficiency and security. In the last two decades, feminist architects and community organizers have formed nonprofit development corporations dedicated to providing women and their children with low-cost housing that also addresses their financial and social needs. These architects, in groups and partnerships, provide advice on forming housing cooperatives; on design, planning, and construction; on negotiations with government agencies and mortgage companies; and on establishing building management and maintenance practices.

The economic development component of housing for low-income single parents (virtually all women) includes the creation of several service businesses based on women's traditional homemaking skills as well as opportunities for nontraditional job training, such as construction. The intention is to provide cost-effective services essential to working mothers that will also generate jobs for some of them, and the development of new skills that will enable all of them to be self-supporting. For example, the program for the rehabilitation of one hundred units of abandoned and underutilized housing in a multi-ethnic neighborhood near Providence, Rhode Island, designed by the Women's Development Corporation in 1978, called for a cafeteria; bakery; food cooperative; clothing and furniture recycling center; daycare cooperative for children, disabled, and aged persons; headquarters where residents could do carpentry; a do-it-yourself automobile repair shop; a solar greenhouse and garden area; workshop and classroom space; recreation area; and rentable work space for related enterprises. The housing in the development, called Villa Excelsior, also created jobs in maintenance and management for some of the residents.

Although many of these ideas were never implemented at Villa Excelsior, seventy-six of the proposed one hundred units were actually built on ten scattered sites (thirty-six in Elmwood and forty units in Mt. Hope) and included new construction, substantially rehabilitated units, and an historic building (see fig. 20). All seventy-six units have been fully occupied since construction was completed in 1983 at a cost of over three million dollars. In 1989, with a few exceptions, all of the households were still headed by women. Residents pay no more than 30 percent of their income for rents; the federal government subsidizes the difference between that amount and the open market price. The thirty-seven two-bedroom units rent for $850 to $900; thirty-six three-bedroom units for $1,000 to $1,100; and the three four-bedroom units for $1,200 to $1,300 per month. Apartment sizes vary from 850 to 1,350 square feet. The Villa Excelsior is still managed by the Women's Development Corporation.[54]

Similar rental apartments are currently being developed by the Women's Research and Development Center in Cincinnati. The

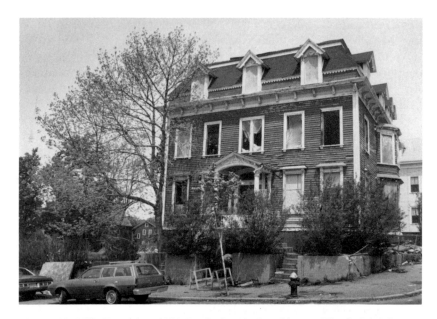

Figure 20. Villa Excelsior, 1208 Doyle Street, Providence, Rhode Island, May 1983, The Women's Development Corporation, architects and developers. One of the abandoned houses targeted for substantial rehabilitation for low-income single mothers by the Women's Development Corporation. Photograph courtesy The Women's Development Corporation.

WRDC was founded in 1988 by women dedicated to creating affordable housing for women. A year later, the organization purchased the Garfield Elementary School from the local school board for one dollar. The brick structure, built in 1889, is located in South Cumminsville, a stable, predominantly black, working-class neighborhood. The WRDC's adaptive re-use plans call for forty-three apartment units of varying sizes—from efficiencies to three bedrooms—for low- to moderate-income single parents and elderly women homeowners living in the neighborhood. Rental space for a childcare provider will also be included at Garfield Commons. A large public park surrounds the site, which is also on a major bus route. Shopping is located within walking distance.

The WRDC has selected the architectural firm of Bowers, Bryan, and Feidt, from St. Paul, Minnesota, to design the housing development, in association with Hefley/Stevens, architects, of Cincinnati. Mary Vogel (the designer of the Women's Advocate's Shelter described in chapter 4) is the project programmer and designer; Dan

Feidt is the project architect. The WRDC raised construction funds from city low-income tax credits, individuals, philanthropic foundations, and religious organizations. Construction is scheduled to begin in December 1991 or in the spring of 1992, and is targeted for completion in summer 1993.[55]

Just as connecting jobs to housing is critical for single women with children, homeownership is crucial as a means of providing a secure base from which to deal with the larger world. Housing stability is especially important to women struggling on their own to make ends meet. Whether owned or rented, housing units for single mothers must be carefully designed with considerable spatial variety to encourage opportunities to congregate and enjoy extended family living without sacrificing privacy. The Women's Development Corporation design prototype located additional rooms or "mini-units" between private units to be used as shared guest space, and created a number of different kitchen-dining arrangements, from compact kitchens in the living area to large eat-in kitchens that serve more than one family.

These concepts of shared space should ideally foster informal, personally supportive relationships among neighbors that are invaluable to adults who lack the support of a spouse or other adult partner. In Dolores Hayden and Ina Dubnoff's design for a housing development for single parents in the Watts/Willowbrook section of Los Angeles (1985–86), the site plan and floorplans were developed to enhance adults' views of children at play, both inside and outside. Intercoms between apartments and connected to bedrooms and kitchens allowed neighbors to babysit while they were not physically present. In addition, individual units were made smaller so that more money could be spent on common areas like garden courtyards.[56]

In another model project, the Constance Hamilton Housing Cooperative in Toronto, a group of women joined forces in 1982 with an architect, Joan Simon, to develop thirty apartment units of one, two, and three bedrooms, with a six-bedroom communal house designed for women leaving hostels or crisis centers (see fig. 21).[57] In 1989, despite some maintenance problems caused by "cost-cutting" construction methods and materials and some personal disagreements among the residents, both the architecture and the cooperative were holding up very well.[58]

These examples of women helping women to house themselves show the kind of comprehensive design and planning needed to enable low-income women to move from poverty and welfare to self-sufficiency, gainful employment, and homeownership. This notion of

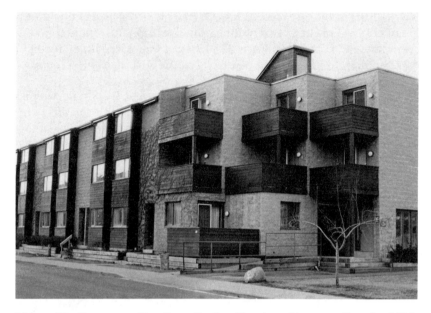

Figure 21. Constance Hamilton Co-Op Housing, Toronto, Canada, 1988, Joan Simon, architect. Constance Hamilton is the first women's housing cooperative built in North America. It contains thirty-one units ranging from one to three bedrooms and a six-bedroom unit of transitional housing for post-crisis women leaving shelters and hostels. Twenty-five percent of the units are rent subsidized. In most cases, living rooms and dining-kitchens are on separate floors, and some bedrooms are downstairs to accommodate the privacy needs of teenagers, adults sharing, and three-generation families. A ground-level communal laundry overlooks the park. Photograph courtesy Pamela L. Sayne.

public and collective responsibility for the quality of domestic life is not utopian idealism, its architectural expression is not fantasy, and the creation of such conditions is not limited to the historical examples mentioned at the beginning of this chapter, or those just described for single parents. Multifamily housing with collective services available for purchase or included in the rent has existed in Sweden for over seventy years. The first *servicehus* was designed by Sven Markelius in collaboration with the internationally known sociologists Alva and Gunnar Myrdal and built in Stockholm in 1907. Since then Sweden has built some twenty or more service houses (also called collective housing or family hotels) which have functioned according to plan for up to thirty years. Like the American feminist models of the past and present, this type of housing offers residents cooked meals from a central kitchen, a communal dining option, laundering, house cleaning, and childcare, plus maternity and well-baby clinics, medical care for the elderly, errand running for the sick, hobby and activity rooms, youth clubs, plant watering during vacations, and gymnasia.[59]

While few governments have been as progressive as Sweden's in developing housing that supports workers and their families, the pressing need for such solutions is obvious. It is essential that we design and plan dwellings and neighborhoods that address changing conditions of family life in a socially responsible way. If we fail to recognize the demographic facts of contemporary household diversity, we will continue to design and build housing in community patterns and densities that more or less suit the traditional, auto-dependent nuclear family that exists today more in myth and nostalgia than in reality.

Designing for Diversity:
The Need for Flexible Architecture

One of the first changes we must incorporate in socially responsible housing is spatial flexibility. Our domestic architecture should be a stage set for various human dramas. It must be demountable, reusable, multifunctional, and changeable over time. No specific arrangement should be typical. But our housing has traditionally included a set of fixed spaces, not fluid ones, and in a fairly predictable and permanent relationship to each other: master bedroom, bath, other bedrooms, living room, perhaps a den or family room, kitchen, dining room, and so on. Each of these enclosed rooms has a particular single function. Room dimensions and the placement of window and door openings are based upon these functions, which in turn determine the layout of furniture. Hallways, stairs, and vestibules are estblished between the different rooms to reinforce zones of privacy and togetherness according to social rules. For example, bedrooms and toilets (considered private) are generally segregated from dining and living rooms (considered public). Electrical, plumbing, and heating systems are located with these factors in mind. Once established by fixed architectural elements, these single-use spaces and zones are not easily converted.

While our homes may remain relatively unchanged over time, our lives do not. We change our work and our relationships, choose partners, bear children, age, and live alone. Yet our homes are designed for two-parent families with children, and a mother in residence to supervise both them and the house. They are not necessarily suitable for "empty nesters," single people, unrelated adults, or dual-career couples. Static, nonflexible housing does not reflect the dynamics of the human life-cycle or the diversity of today's households.

In 1984 Katrin Adam and Barbara Marks, two architects, proposed a scheme for the development of housing for homeless women and single-parent families in three buildings formerly owned by Greenpoint Hospital in Brooklyn, New York. They designed the buildings to encourage self-sufficiency, afford possibilities for interdependent "extended family" living, and provide flexibility within the units that could accommodate diverse household patterns. While minimal financial and family resources often force women to share housing that is not designed for this purpose, Adam and Marks's carefully planned series of floor layouts and unit types offers varying degrees of privacy and sharing that recognizes differing needs and preferences of individuals and families. For example, the second-floor plan of Building 8 (fig. 22) includes a common space with toilet outside the private apartments and adjacent to shared laundry facilities (center top) that can be used for social gatherings, a children's play area, an office or workshop, or a guest bedroom. The unit on the top right of the plan is designed as a three-bedroom family apartment that incorporates a private efficiency unit for a related or unrelated person who can share in family life and responsibility while maintaining an independent lifestyle. In the apartment unit on the left of the plan, the large eat-in kitchen is designed as the family gathering place, while the smaller living room can be used either for formal and intimate socializing or as a fourth bedroom. The third-floor plan of Building 8 (fig. 23) provides a two-family apartment (center top) in which each family has its own entry, bath, and three bedrooms, with a common living room and kitchen in which only the stove is shared. Private refrigerators, sinks, and storage cabinets clarify the boundaries and responsibilities for each household's tastes and standards in quantity and type of food, cooking, and cleanup. This arrangement could be particularly supportive to working women with children. The first-floor plan of Building 8 (not illustrated) contains a centrally located porch, a lounge, and an eat-in kitchen to be shared by all the residents of the building for group dining, meetings, childcare, and parties, and one- and two-bedroom apartments that are wheelchair accessible.

As Adam and Marks's housing scheme demonstrates, a home established for a family with young children must be modifiable by family members as they change and grow. Each household must be able

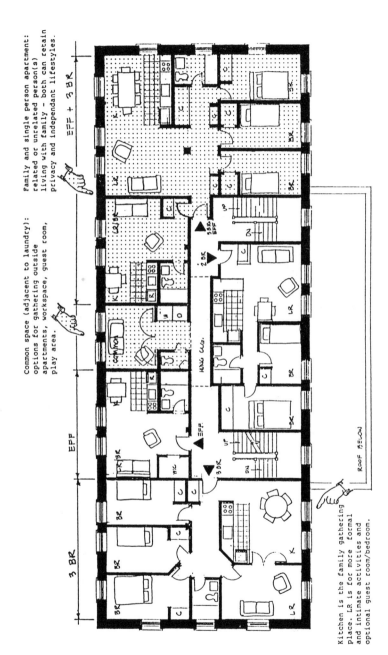

Family and single person apartment: related or unrelated person(s) living with family – both can retain privacy and independant lifestyles.

Common space (adjacent to laundry): options for gathering outside apartments, workspace, guest room, play area.

Kitchen is the family gathering place. LR is for more formal and intimate activities and optional guest room/bedroom.

EFF + 3 BR

EFF

3 BR

2ND FLOOR PLAN – BLDG. 8

Figures 22 and 23. Neighborhood Women's Inter-Generational Housing, Greenpoint, Brooklyn, New York, 1984, Katrin Adam with Barbara Marks, architects, National Congress of Neighborhood Women, client. Drawings courtesy Katrin Adam, architect.

2 family apartment: each family has own entry, bath and bedrooms. Shared large living room, common kitchen in which only the stove is shared.

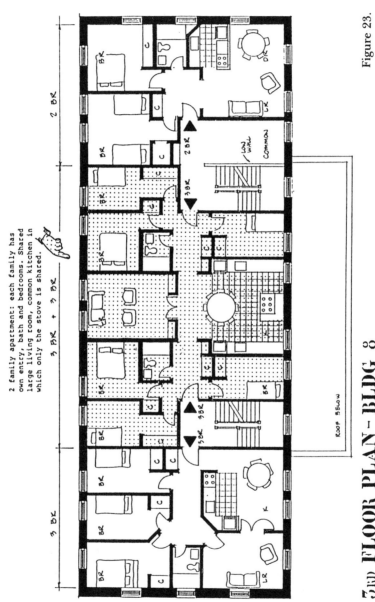

3RD FLOOR PLAN - BLDG 8

Figure 23.

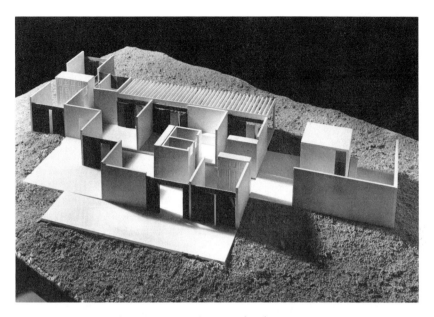

Figure 24. House in Santo Domingo, 1972–73, Susana Torre, architect. Model with roof removed, front view. This 1,400-square-foot house was designed for an extended family consisting of a couple and the wife's mother and younger sister. Because their lives are both joined and separate, Torre paired the private rooms of each household at opposite ends of the house. The main connecting space is a series of three rooms in a zigzag pattern, which can be divided in many different ways by large sliding doors. The structure in the laundry yard to the right of the car entrance, used as a workshop and office by the mother, a seamstress, was designed to become the starting place for future additions once the younger sister establishes her own separate but connected household. Photograph by Stan Ries, reproduced courtesy Susana Torre, architect.

to "arrange" its own domestic space so that it functions well specifically for them, and can be changed again when it does not. The relationships in a "voluntary family" of unrelated single adults of the same or opposite sex are often very different from those of married couples. The spatial organization and use in each household's respective dwelling should express those differences.

Our homes must become places in which the residents can share the responsibilities and where housework is no longer specialized and demeaning, but an obvious and integrated part of each person's daily life. Kitchens will have to be redesigned to accommodate several cooks at the same or different times, and these cooks should include children and guests. Equipment must be visually and physically accessible to everyone, as in a restaurant kitchen. People need not experience the frustration that accompanies trying to work in someone else's kitchen, where they cannot find anything because it was designed for the exclusive use of one person—usually a housewife.

Within the dwelling, the relationship, size, and use of various rooms must become less specific. We must abandon the current nomenclature of rooms because names like "family room" and "master bedroom" restrict our ability to visualize and subsequently actualize a more flexible use of space.[60] Spaces must lend themselves equally well to sleeping, living, and working, to being used privately or shared, to expanding and contracting in size and shape. Permanent walls can be replaced with sliding screens, modular partitions that clip in or swing in and out, folding wall panels, and "curtains" of vinyl, wood, metal, and fabric.

These ideas are not untested fantasies. Many European countries, particularly Holland, Germany, and France, have experimented with housing systems designed to adapt to social change. Stichting Architectin Research (SAR) in Holland is one example. SAR philosophy embraces the belief that dwelling is more than physical shelter, it is a human act. Architects involved in SAR research "guide" the future tenants of their housing complexes in designing their own living spaces, which are spatially adaptable to meet the needs of household conditions and new residents. For example, one family living in Molenvliet, a project designed by Frans Van der Werf containing 122 units at a density of 37 dwellings per acre, lowered the windowsills in their living area to provide the severely disabled father with a view from his wheelchair.

A structural support system of concrete piers combined with infill consisting of an assembly kit of non-load-bearing walls, vertical service ducts, doors, stairs, kitchen units, bathrooms, and changeable elements on the facade allow alterations in the spatial arrangements of rooms, their sizes, and the amount of natural light admitted. Partitions can be removed by loosening a screw fitting; plumbing is accessible and electrical wiring is surface-mounted in base and ceiling moldings. Skilled labor is required only for modifications to the central heating system and bathroom tile. Housing projects based on SAR principles have been built in Austria, England, and the United States (in California), in addition to Holland.[61]

Several other projects based on tenant participation were built by committed disciples of the Dutch designer N. J. Habraken, who, in his book *Supports: An Alternative to Mass Housing* (1964), criticized the totalitarian, impersonal mass housing estates built in Europe after World War II. He proposed using industrialized structural frameworks that tenants could personalize through selecting interior walls, equipment, and finishes from a wide array of manufactured products.[62]

Other examples are found in Denmark where, in 1973, the first *bofaelleskab*—a term which literally means "livingtogetherness"—was founded by twenty-seven families. By 1988 about seventy more had been built. Ranging from six to eighty households, they are urban and rural, owned and rented. These co-housing communities are designed by their residents, in constant collaboration with architects and technical advisors, to anticipate changes in family structure and to provide flexibility for couples, nuclear families, singles, single parents, and retirees. At Gaglebakken, some units have walls that can be moved and a family expecting a child can acquire a new room from a neighbor by changing the wall configuration. At Sol og Vind, where communal living is emphasized, thirty homes form one enclosed unit in which families live on either side of an interior glass-roofed hallway of nonuniform walls reminiscent of medieval streets. The "interior street" serves as a large living and recreation space for adults and children. Many *bofaelleskabs* have separate rooms for teenagers. To save on costs, residents generally select plain construction materials like prefabricated concrete columns and slabs, unstained wood, and corrugated panels that create a utilitarian look. Still, the initial higher cost of user participation in the design of the housing means that most residents will, of necessity, be higher-income professionals. The same has proven to be true in the United States where co-housing is currently being promoted by the architects Kathryn McCamant and Charles Durrett.[63]

In addition to spatial flexibility, our homes must offer us economic flexibility. If housing is to become affordable, units will no doubt have to become smaller and higher in density, but not necessarily less comfortable, functional, or private as a result. Many of the rooms we now have in large homes are infrequently used. In new condominium and cluster-style housing developments we could shift guest bedrooms, for example, from each individual dwelling unit to nearby locations within the development itself, where they can be reserved for the occasional visitor. We could cut down on the size of individual living rooms by providing large community rooms with kitchens to be rented out by tenants or owners for big gatherings. A successful variation of this approach to creating affordable housing has been developed for single people and single parents of all ages by Innovative

Housing, a nonprofit, San Francisco-based organization. There, "vest pocket communities" consist of twelve to twenty small cottages and studio apartments of between 250 and 400 square feet with minimal private kitchen facilities, clustered around more expensive shared amenities for cooking, dining, and working.[64]

Costs can be further reduced by "do-it-yourself" housing. Prepackaged and component housing is already available to the nonprofessional, from walls with pre-installed wiring and plumbing to complete kitchens and entire "dream houses" sold with blueprints and instruction manuals. People should also be able to buy new housing built to different degrees of completion that they can finish themselves. However, at present, lending institutions do not favor such proposals. They worry that if they are forced to repossess a house that has been designed or built by an amateur, it will be too eccentric or poorly constructed to be easily resold. But these problems are not insolvable.

The biggest obstacle we face in developing pluralistic, flexible housing is not design, technology, or even the profit motive, it is our own attitude. If we are to implement new ideas, we will first have to recognize how conceptually disadvantaged we all are by the immutable social and architectural preconceptions we have about our housing and our households. Then we will have to find ways to free ourselves of the inhibitions they cause.

NOTES

The opening epigraph is from Charlotte Perkins Gilman, "The Passing of the Home in Great American Cities," *Cosmopolitan,* December 1904, reprinted in *Heresies,* issue 11, vol. 3, no. 3 (1981): 55.

1. The most complete documentation of feminist proposals for revolutionizing the American home and neighborhood as a means of establishing women's equality can be found in Dolores Hayden's seminal work, *The Grand Domestic Revolution: A History of Feminist Designs for American Homes, Neighborhoods, and Cities* (Cambridge: MIT Press, 1981).

2. The Women, Public Policy and Development Project of the Hubert H. Humphrey Institute of Public Affairs, University of Minnesota, "Worker, Mother, Wife" (unpublished paper, August 1984).

3. Wright, *Building the Dream,* 279.

4. Statistics were obtained from the following sources: *A Statistical Portrait of Women in the United States: 1978,* Current Population Series—Special Studies P-23, no. 100 (Washington, D.C.: U.S. Department of Commerce, Bureau of the Census, August 1978); *Women Today* 12, issue 6 (22 March 1982): 34; *Washington Women's Representative* 5, no. 16 (31 August 1980): 2; Betty

Friedan, "Feminism Takes a New Turn," *New York Times Magazine,* 18 November 1979, 92; William Severini Kowinski, "Suburbia: End of the Golden Age," *New York Times Magazine,* 16 March 1980, 17.

5. Friedan, "Feminism Takes a New Turn," 92.

6. Jo Freeman, "Women and Urban Policy," *Signs,* special issue, "Women and the City," supplement, vol. 5, no. 3 (Spring 1980): 15.

7. Lois Scharf, *To Work and to Wed: Female Employment, Feminism, and the Great Depression,* cited in the *New Women's Times Feminist Review* (May-June 1982): 8.

8. Elise Boulding, *Women: The Fifth World,* Headline Series 248 (New York: Foreign Policy Association, February 1980), 13.

9. Boulding, *Underside of History,* 554.

10. Ibid., 496.

11. Aptheker, *Women's Legacy,* 132.

12. Ibid., 135–36.

13. Ibid., 133.

14. George Masnick, *The Nation's Families: 1960–1990* (Boston: Auburn House, 1980), 48.

15. John Hancock, "The Apartment House in Urban America," in *Essays on the Social Development of the Built Environment,* ed. Anthony D. King (London: Routledge and Kegan Paul, 1980), 157.

16. Kowinski, "Suburbia," 106.

17. Karen A. Franck, "Together or Apart: Sharing and the American Household," unpublished paper, New Jersey Institute of Technology (1985).

18. Quoted from Mildred F. Schmertz, "Round Table, Housing and Community Design for Changing Family Needs," *Architectural Record* (December 1979).

19. Dolores Barclay, "More Landlords Rejecting Kids," report distributed by the Children's Defense and Education Fund, Washington, D.C., undated, unpaginated.

20. Toni Klimberg, "Excluding the Commune from Suburbia: The Use of Zoning for Social Control," *Hastings Law Journal* 23 (May 1972): 1461.

21. Ibid.

22. James A. Smith, Jr., "Burning the House to Roast the Pig: Unrelated Individuals and Single Family Zoning's Blood Relation Criteria," *Cornell Law Review* 58 (1972): 146.

23. Nancy Rubin, *The New Suburban Woman: Beyond Myth and Motherhood* (New York: Coward, McCann, and Geoghegan, 1982), 191.

24. Wright, *Building the Dream,* 247.

25. Ibid.

26. Ibid., 248.

27. Toni Klimberg, "Excluding the Commune from Suburbia," 1471.

28. Ibid.

29. Smith, "Burning the House," 153.

30. Ibid., 149.

31. Kowinski, "Suburbia," 19.

32. Anthony De Palma, "Mount Laurel: Slow, Painful Progress," *New York Times*, 1 May 1988, section 10, pp. 1, 20.

33. Ibid., 20.

34. Gerda R. Wekerle, "Urban Planning: Making It Work for Women," *Status of Women News*, "The Environment: A Feminist Issue," 6, no. 3 (Winter 1979–80): 3.

35. Ronald F. Gatti, "Radburn, the Town for the Motor Age," unpublished paper made available through the Radburn Association, 2920 Fairlawn Avenue, Fairlawn, New Jersey 07410. For more information also see Henry Wright, Jr., "Radburn Revisited," *Architectural Forum* (July/August 1971): 52–57, and Clarence Stein, *Toward New Towns for America* (Cambridge: MIT Press, 1957, 1971).

36. Interview with Ernest Morris, longtime Radburn resident and past president of the Radburn Senior Citizens Club, 11 February 1987.

37. Dolores Hayden, "What Would a Non-Sexist City Be Like? Speculation on Housing, Urban Design, and Human Work," *Signs* 5, no. 3 (Spring 1980): S170–87.

38. Patrick Hare, "Reforming Traditional Zoning" (Lecture delivered at the Fourth Annual UCLA Graduate School of Architecture and Urban Planning Conference, Women's Issues: Planning for Women and the Changing Household, University of California, Los Angeles, 24 April 1982).

39. Frances Cerra, "Ones and Twos Becoming Illegal Threes," *New York Times*, 27 February 1983, section 8, p. 1.

40. Sylvia Porter, "Why You Can't Afford to Buy and Keep a House," *New York Daily News*, 25 October 1981, Business section, p. 59; Kowinski, "Suburbia," 17.

41. Walter Updegrave, "Locked Out! The Housing Crisis Hits Home," *Metropolitan Home*, October 1989, 104.

42. Hare, "Reforming Traditional Zoning."

43. Wright, *Building the Dream*, 279.

44. Hare, "Reforming Traditional Zoning."

45. Lenore Weitzman, *The Divorce Revolution* (New York: Free Press, 1985).

46. Susan Anderson-Khleif, "Housing Needs of Single Parent Mothers," *Building for Women*, ed. Keller, 25–26.

47. Howard S. Shapiro and Emilie Lounsberry, "Hard Times Forcing Grown Children Back to the Nest," *The Sunday Camera* (New Jersey), 13 March 1983, section D, 1.

48. Markson and Hess, "Older Women in the City," 130.

49. Gray Panthers, "Age and Youth . . . Together for a Change," offset fact sheet, undated, unpaginated.

50. *Women Today*, 22 March 1982, 34.

51. Markson and Hess, "Older Women in the City," 136.

52. Melinda Beck, "The Geezer Boom," *Newsweek*, special issue, "The 21st-Century Family," Winter/Spring 1990, 66.

53. Ibid., 62–63.

54. Katrin Adam, Susan E. Aitcheson, and Joan Forrester Sprague, "Women's Development Corporation," *Heresies*, "Making Room: Women and Architecture," issue 11, vol. 3, no. 3 (1981): 19–20; interview with Susan E. Aitcheson, Development Director, and Alma Felix Green, President, Women's Development Corporation, August 1989. For more information contact WDC at 861A Broad Street, Providence, Rhode Island 02907.

55. For more information about the Women's Research and Development Center or Garfield Commons, contact Maureen Wood, Executive Director, 727 Ezzard Charles Drive, Cincinnati, Ohio 45203; phone (513) 721–1841.

56. Karen A. Franck, "At Home in the Future: Feminist Visions and Some Built Examples," unpublished paper, New Jersey Institute of Technology, 1986.

57. For more information write to Lyn Adamsun, Constance Hamilton Housing Co-operative, 523 Melita Cr., Toronto, Ontario, Canada.

58. For the most recent information on housing projects by and for women in Canada, see Gerda R. Wekerle, *Women's Housing Projects in Eight Canadian Cities* (Toronto: Canada Housing and Mortgage Corporation, 1988), and for those in the United States see Karen A. Franck and Sherry Ahrentzen, eds., *New Households, New Housing* (New York: Van Nostrand Reinhold, 1989).

59. This description and summary of the history of collective housing in Sweden is based on two articles: Dick Urban Vestbro, "Collective Housing Units in Sweden," *Women and Environments* 4, no. 3 (December 1980–January 1981): 8–9; and Ellen Perry Berkeley, "The Swedish Servicehus," *Architecture Plus* (May 1973): 56–59.

60. In 1930, architect Elisabeth Coit advanced this position in her landmark housing studies. See Elisabeth Coit, "Notes on the Design and Construction of the Dwelling Units for the Lower-Income Family," *The Octagon* (October 1941): 10–30, and (November 1941): 7–22.

61. C. Richard Hatch, *The Scope of Social Architecture* (New York: Van Nostrand Reinhold, 1979), 23, 32, 35.

62. Nicholas John Habraken, *Supports: An Alternative to Mass Housing* (Cambridge, Mass.: MIT Press, 1964).

63. Roberto Diaz and Amy Kates, "Livingtogetherness in Denmark," *Colloqui, A Journal of Planning and Urban Issues*, special issue, "The Family" (Spring, 1987): 4–7. For comprehensive information on Danish co-housing, see Kathryn McCamant and Charles Durret, *Co-Housing, A Contemporary Approach to Housing Ourselves* (Berkeley: Habitat Press, 1988).

64. Ellisa Dennis, "Shared Housing: An Innovative Approach," *Shelterforce* 12, no. 1 (July–September 1989): 12–15.

6

At Home in the Future

I start to imagine
plans for a house, a park . . .
A city waits at the back of my skull
eating its heart out to be born:
how design the first
city of the moon? How shall I see it
for all of us who are done with enclosed
spaces, purdah, the salon,
the sweat loft, the ingenuity of the cloister?

—Adrienne Rich
"The Fourth Month of the
Landscape Architect"

In thinking about the future it is perfectly reasonable to ask, Can we establish homes in which all women can lead fully independent lives? Where housework and nurturance have nothing to do with gender? Where children are taught to believe in human potential, not gender roles? Where they are raised by nuclear families and families of choice; by men, old people, and chosen parents as well as women and their biological parents?

Visualizing such a radically different future is not easy. When we fantasize we usually imagine some "improved" version of our present realities. Our ability to imagine a future free of sexism, racism, and classism is to some extent a function of the degree to which it already exists. But to the extent that we can create nonsexist visions of the future, we begin to overcome contemporary sexism. In architectural terms, that means that we cannot easily conceive of "housing for liberated people" while we live in a sexist society, but to the degree that we can, we are reshaping tomorrow's housing by reshaping ourselves today.

The future that we and our children will live in can be a SHE future or a HE future (terms coined by James Robertson, a futurist). The SHE future is sane, human, ecological; its new frontiers are psychological and social, not technical and economic. In the SHE future the development of people, not the development of things, will be important. The HE future envisions a hyperexpansionist, industrial, high-technology way of life, dependent upon advanced science to extend material growth in areas like space colonization, nuclear energy, and genetic engineering. In the HE future, personal care and social services will be increasingly institutionalized and professionalized.[1]

How might housing and households look in each of these contrasting futures? To make the comparison vivid, I have selected examples written in the 1980s that already seem dated, as with the predicted dramatic impact of the home computer on domestic life, while other scenarios written by feminists in the early 1970s, describing dwellings designed on the principles of equality of human worth and individual autonomy, still seem like radically distant dreams. I do not assume here that the HE or the SHE future, and the values embodied in each, are gender exclusive. Rather, by projecting ourselves into both "pictures" of the future, we can begin to experience and see the world more clearly, as it is, and as it could be.

The first "picture" of the HE future comes from an article on optical data transmission and high-speed computers that appeared in *Science Digest* in April 1983. Explaining that our communications technology has shifted from "low gear to warp drive," the author predicted that "by the year 2000 the result will be a world profoundly different from the one we find today." To illustrate, he "zooms in on an average family in the year 2000":

> Mark Bentley, a pump designer for Fusion International, will spend today working from home. He has no real reason to go to the plant when all he has to do is discuss the new pump drawings with the review board. That can just as easily be handled over the videocom. Besides, he wants to spend some extra time with his family today. The terminal will be available all day, since Mark's wife Tiffany is able to use the family's other terminal to do the shopping and update the children's monthly physicals. It will be a bit inconvenient for eight-year-old Mark Jr., who also needs the terminal for his music lesson and a math test, and for his older sister, who wants to study with her friends. But somehow Tiffany has it all worked out.[2]

Tiffany, you will observe, is still smoothing the ruffled feathers in her nuclear family nest, tending to the children, and worrying about what to buy for dinner, although she can do the shopping from her cozy, ivy-covered, electronic bungalow. And how will the computerized cottage of the future liberate the "working" wife and mother? Alvin Toffler joyfully proclaimed in *The Third Wave* (1981) that home computers would enable secretaries to work at home where they could tend their small children. Not surprisingly, Toffler made no reference to men working at home sharing childcare.[3]

Another example of the "profoundly different world" of the HE future comes from *Mechanix Illustrated,* January 1981, in an article on robotics: "Homes will be . . . robots, with a centralized computer doing the thinking and . . . will handle household chores ranging from vacuuming to mowing the lawn. . . . The central computer will keep an inventory of household supplies, down to the salt and pepper, and order them when they get low. . . . If the Ms. of the household should cook some exotic dish, she could feed the recipe to the robot and it would gather the ingredients, ordering anything which happened not to be on hand."[4] The "Ms." of this household is hardly a liberated woman; and if she knows what's good for her, she will find Tiffany and start a consciousness-raising group.

We should not be fooled by the perfidious visions of a liberated future filled with technological gadgetry. Such visions are nothing more than patriarchal sophistry. Certainly technology has eliminated much of the arduous physical strain of household and industrial labor. But it has never freed women or men from the confinement of gender roles.

For generations, men have tried to convince women that the conspicuous consumption of "labor-saving devices" would free them from the boring exhaustion of housework. In the 1930s, the corporate campaign to promote the gadget-filled, wired-up dream kitchen as the hallmark of "modern living" centered around the motto "Electricity Is Her Servant."[5] Today the rhetoric is much the same but the language of domestic liberation is "computerese."

There is no doubt that by the year 2000 computer literacy will be an essential skill. People who are unable to use computers will live in a state of information poverty, excluded from many day-to-day activities, and certainly excluded from power, according to Jan Zimmerman, a communications expert. Zimmerman agrees that the home computer could ease housework, reduce the time spent in running errands, support shared parenting responsibilities, and offer countless other benefits to women, men, and families. But she concludes with the following caveat: "Women could use computers . . . or computers could use women, just as other technologies have. . . . The substitution of electronic communication for face-to-face contact may reisolate women in the home. . . . Women may find themselves once again prisoners of gilded suburban cages, their feet bound by copper cable, optical fiber, and the invisible chains of electromagnetic waves."[6] Further, the use of home computers to pay bills, order groceries, and do research threatens to eliminate paying jobs that women have traditionally filled, from bank teller and grocery clerk to book-keeper and librarian.

The HE future, focused on technology, looks much the same for women as the HE present (see fig. 25). The robot, home computer, and "smart house" will do little more for women's liberation than the vacuum cleaner and televison have done. The male engineers at work computerizing the house, in failing to acknowledge households based on models other than the nuclear family, are replicating in the future the domestic conditions that have comforted men in the past.

What would be different in the SHE future? In 1973 the anthro-pologist Margaret Mead wrote: "The first thing we have to get rid of is this horrible independent little misery called the surburban home. It is using up an unprecedented amount of hardware, creating an un-precedented amount of pollution, and producing unhappy people."[7] In 1981 Betty Friedan agreed: "It is that physical, literal house . . . that keeps us from transcending those old sex roles that too often have locked us in mutual misery in the family. I keep remembering that . . . isolated house with all those appliances each woman had to spend all day operating by herself; somehow [it] made us spend more time doing housework than our mothers and grandmothers—and drove our husbands to ulcers or premature heart attacks in the rat race to pay for them."[8]

But what are the alternatives? The measures discussed in the pre-vious chapter, such as reforming single-family zoning, legalizing ac-cessory apartments, and providing community services like child and elder care and public laundries, should be forcefully supported be-cause they are urgently needed. But do not mistake them for "solu-tions." In the long run they will not gain women their equality or change men's relationship to domestic life, for they largely ignore the underlying values that created the problems in the first place. Genuinely satisfying alternatives to conventional housing and com-munities will emerge only as we are able to visualize scenarios of the future based on the reconceptualization of work, family life, and gen-der roles.

In chapter 3 I discussed the notions of equality and equity in rela-tionship to public space. It is appropriate here to examine the impli-cations of housing equality versus housing equity in relationship to the future. The former is symbolized in the familiar American dream, the idealization of the traditional family, the suburban house, home-ownership, conformity. The latter suggests a very different dream in which the person, not the family, is recognized as the basic unit of

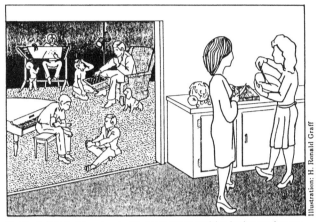

Multi-adult living groups provide many opportunities for human interaction. Two women work and chat in the kitchen while other members of the household engage in recreation and hobby activities. The author states that children, in particular, benefit from the enriched environment found in multi-adult living groups.

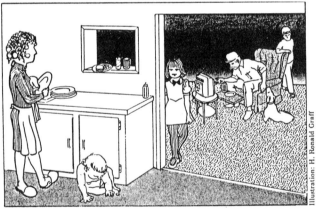

A nuclear family provides only a small number of people to interact with, hence most activities tend to be individualistic. The breadwinner-father, home from work, relaxes with a glass of beer and watches his favorite sportscast while the homemaker-mother prepares dinner. The children, home from school, seem to be searching for someone to interact with.

Figure 25. These illustrations and captions appeared in an article by James Ramey, "Multi-Adult Households: Living Groups of the Future," *The Futurist* (April 1976): 82–83. Even in the nonnuclear families of the "radical future" (top) women and men are engaged in the same traditional work and family roles that characterized the 1970s (bottom) and that continued throughout the 1980s despite the dramatic increase in the numbers of women working for wages full time. Illustrations by H. Ronald Graff, reproduced courtesy The World Future Society.

society—where putative spousal support is replaced by the support of a larger "social family" that offers its help to every woman, man, and child in accordance with their different needs. The following "pictures" of housing and communities in the SHE future describe how these values might be architecturally expressed.

Housing and Human Liberation

At home with the women
Under the full sail of their abilities
I count my fingers and wish them buildings
I count my legs and wish them hammers
I count my arms and wish them bulldozers
I look into my eyes and wish them geometry
I look into my head and wish it a compass
I look into my heart and wish it architecture
I look into my womb and wish I had designed it.
(Frances Whyatt, "The Craft
of Their Hands")[9]

In *The Dialectic of Sex: The Case for Feminist Revolution* (1970), Shulamith Firestone proposed replacing the biological/legal family with the household, defined as a "large group of people living together for an unspecific time with no specific interpersonal relationships." These households would live in a complex the size of a small town or a large campus: "We could have small units of self-determined housing—prefabricated component parts set up or dismantled easily and quickly . . . as well as central permanent buildings to fill the needs of the community as a whole, i.e. perhaps the equivalent of a 'student union' for socializing, restaurants, a large computer bank, a modern communications center . . . and whatever else might be necessary in a cybernetic community."[10]

The university setting with its transient population and combination of adjacent living, work, and social spaces was a logical model to use as a basis for proposing alternative communities in the 1970s, a decade of political protest and campus demonstrations. In 1972, Craig, Kent, and Vicki Hodgetts devised a more elaborate campus plan which they hailed as the "birth of individual architecture." Their mobile campsite system was to be built over existing suburban tract sites. In their "liberated communities" every man, woman, and child over the age of six or seven was autonomous. Each person was provided a private bedroom, studio, kitchen, and bath. Microwave ovens that never got hot were safe for use by children who chose to live alone. These campsites could be clustered together and moved apart to make new forms. Rooms could be added and changed for any purpose and to any size through a system of walls suspended from ceiling tracks in corridors that linked separate units. Two people might live together by opening up the corridor area between their own units to make a private house. Three or four people could do the same. Public shops, theaters, classrooms, libraries, infant care, and so on were located on intersecting corridors.[11] This visionary scheme for individual architecture is not at all farfetched. As discussed in the previous chapter, the necessary building technologies already exist.

Other feminist activists writing in the 1970s believed that women could gain autonomy only by living exclusively with each other. A spokeswoman for *The Ladder*, a radical feminist publication, suggested that "a society in which women are liberated in their environment would be a maleless or womanpowered society and would have little to do with architecture."[12] Germaine Greer countered with the argument that the all-woman commune was positive for women in the personal sense but useless in the political sense: "It is in no way different from the medieval convents where women who revolted against their social and biological roles could achieve intellectual and moral fulfillment from which they exerted no pressure on the status quo at all."[13]

Mary Daly, a feminist theologian, disagreed with Greer. "The process [of a women's revolution]," wrote Daly, "involves the creation of new space in which women are free to become who we are, and in which there are real and significant alternatives to the identities provided within the enclosed spaces of patriarchal institutions."[14] Daly maintained that the establishment of separatist space for women was more than comforting escapism, it was a radically political act.

Separatism has been construed as "man-hating" at worst and a rejection of men at best. Sometimes each is true, but not always. Separatism is also about choosing to live with women, a choice made by both lesbians and heterosexual women in the 1960s, in cities and suburbs worldwide, as a direct spinoff of the women's movement. Many of the women who formed women-only collectives had lived in mixed communities but found them intolerably male-dominated. In the 1960s, other collectives for both women and men were founded in which gender roles were abandoned, like Findhorn in Scotland (1962) and Twin Oaks in Virginia (1966), where there are lesbians, bisexual, and heterosexual women; motherhood and childhood are "community matters" and fathers have as much contact with children as do mothers. Both communities continue to operate today.[15]

Be they real experiments or fictional narratives, communities designed to support human equality must encourage domestic arrangements in which any person or group of people can live with whomever they choose, for whatever duration or purpose, be it political, economic, social, religious, and/or sexual. So too must the conformity and anonymity that currently characterize institutional space be replaced with cooperation among autonomous individuals, as in this description by Tish Sommers of a nursing home in the SHE future:

> The Last Perch [will be] a live-in community of compatible people, some ambulatory and others living their last days in a joyous and beautiful setting. The key difference from present institutions is that the Perchers will hold onto control of their environment. They will select who is to be admitted, what type of food is served, what drinks are available at the bar, what the decor and social arrangements will be, as well as who will be admitted to study them in exchange for specific services. They will have access to a printing press, and a computer, of course, and perhaps they will produce their own television show. Their beautiful cooperative gardens will surround their last years with flowers.[16]

Sommers also suggests that the SHE future will include intergenerational neighborhood co-ops, shared living arrangements among persons needing care; new families of two or more people who share resources, goals, values, and lifestyles instead of blood relationships, legal ties, or marriage; cities with enormous roof solariums to benefit from solar heat and to augment local home gardens and food processing; and the United States Unarmed Services, an organization that recruits unemployed people of all ages to work on energy conservation projects.[17]

At present, perhaps the richest source of writing about a futuristic nonsexist scenario like the one Sommers offers is in feminist science fiction. Authors such as Ursula Le Guin, Joanna Russ, and Marge Piercy vividly describe fictional communities characterized by radical egalitarianism in which power hierarchies are abolished, genetic technology has freed human reproduction from the biology of gender (babies are born *ex utero,* and hermaphrodites can be both mothers and fathers), and all people, including children, are fully independent and equally valued by virtue of their human-ness. Within these imaginative societies, sexual, economic, family, and male/female relationships are artfully redesigned and plants, animals, humans, and the earth live in ecological harmony.[18]

However, while social and metaphysical space are meticulously restructured in these literary works, built space is rendered vaguely if at all. Why? Perhaps because our "rational" Western culture retards the spatial imagination we naturally possess in early childhood, when the world is largely sensate and nonverbal. Young children communicate without inhibition through crayon drawings and structures made of alphabet blocks. They are the architects of sand castles, snow fortresses, and tree houses. As we learn to read, write, and speak, our reliance on drawings and three-dimensional models of the world diminishes. By the time we are adults, if we try to draw in order to express an idea, we usually do so with apology and embarrassment since the results are often"childishly crude."

The widespread use of inexpensive cameras has further removed people from direct, intimate contact with their physical surroundings. People no longer "make" pictures of memorable places and events; they "take" pictures of them. People's ability to be spatially articulate is further thwarted by the fact that physical space is so difficult to describe in words. The cliché "one picture is worth a thousand words" is altogether accurate. Under these circumstances, it is understandable why feminist science-fiction writers expend relatively little of their creative imagination on inventing the physical structures and communities their new societies might build to house themselves and the feminist values they espouse.

Women's Environmental Fantasies

To increase women's awareness of the importance of built space as an expression of social relations, in 1974 I joined Noel Phyllis Birkby in a two-year collaboration in which we asked women to draw their environmental fantasies in workshops we conducted across the United States. The participants were chosen to be diverse in age, lifestyle, experience, and education.[19] Birkby, who originated the project, and I approached this experiment from different and complementary perspectives, she as an architect whose feminism had made her critically aware of the male-dominated nature of architecture and her own professional education, I as a teacher of architecture whose understanding of the ways in which knowledge is defined, created, and learned had been transformed by feminism.

From the start, traditional scholarly research was never a consideration. Rather, we wanted to create a forum for environmental consciousness-raising where women could describe and openly discuss their environmental experiences—the things that frustrated, thwarted, and delimited their activities; those that enhanced and supported their daily lives; and finally, what they would ideally include in their physical surroundings in a world of their own design. We asked our workshop participants to make drawings because graphic communication is well suited to describing the spatial world. We emphasized the drawing process as a means of personal exploration and de-emphasized the visual appearance of the final results.

We encouraged the women to fantasize because we believed in the power of dreams as a force for social and personal change—an important goal of the women's movement. Even though we are taught that fantasy is an impractical waste of time and daydreaming a form of laziness, fantasy dwells within us all. It is a source of primary creativity, invention, and problem solving, not an idle escape from reality. Looking deeply inward to the unconstrained visual landscape of our fantasies helps us to imagine alternatives to adapting to unsuitable space and raises our environmental expectations. As one workshop participant explained it: "If it's your fantasy and you're given permission to fantasize . . . and approval for doing it, it doesn't have to conform to anything. That kind of opportunity for freedom really lets people unleash and get at their true feelings and needs. It's non-judgmental. It's non-intellectual."[20]

Birkby and I collected hundreds of drawings from the workshops we held at feminist conferences, meetings of women's organizations, and sessions of the Women's School of Planning and Architecture (WSPA), a national summer program we cofounded in 1974 with five other women (see Acknowledgments, and Introduction, note 5). Between fifteen and sixty women attended any given workshop. They were mostly, but not all, white women, ranging in age from late teens to early seventies. The majority were between twenty-five and forty-five and well educated; many had earned college degrees. Most were employed or looking for work; only a small percentage were full-time homemakers.

Workshop participants entered a room in which long rolls of paper and a large supply of colored markers stretched across the floor. We instructed the women to get comfortable, close their eyes, and imagine their ideal living environment. With long pauses in between, we asked: "What does it look like?" "What size and shape?" "What is it made of?" "Where is it located?" "What do you do there?" "Is there anyone else there?" "Where?" and so on. As pictures came to mind, the women silently began to draw, allowing their images to develop by free association. After twenty to thirty minutes, they stopped and looked at each other's sketches. Then each woman in turn talked about her experience of the process, the meaning of her own drawing, and how both did or did not relate to those of other participants.

We usually tape-recorded these conversations. The following was typical of many comments: "Underlying the fantasies is a common kind of understanding. I know the sources from which these needs arise. I feel them too, I can relate to the messages in these drawings because I've experienced so many of the same frustrations or needs or daydreams. They make me feel really connected to other women."[21]

As our collection of drawings grew, we began to notice patterns that spoke of shared experiences and common aspirations among the participants. Four "themes" emerged: the women needed private, safe space; they wanted control over who could enter it, why, and for how long; they wanted the physical arrangement of their dwellings to adjust to changes in their moods, activities, and relationships with others; and they felt that it was important to have contact with nature and natural materials that soothe and stimulate the senses.

For example, one woman described her fantasy dwelling as a "totally open circular prism of color surrounded by trees and daffodils" where she and her husband lived "each in their own dream structures." Another woman's organic "snail house" grew according to phases in the human life-cycle, from birth to retirement. A third woman drew a "very soft house that flies and can go anywhere, will grow and have new rooms every time I think of a new project to work on and includes a very special feature: all rooms magically clean themselves."[22] (Figures 26 through 30 illustrate other imaginative ways these themes were visually expressed.)

A number of factors likely biased these fantasy drawings. The drawing process took place in a supportive context where participants were encouraged to fantasize about nonsexist, nurturant environments that supported their needs. If we had asked participants to imagine their dream house instead of their ideal fantasy environment, more would have been inclined to produce variations of the single-family house. If we had obtained more drawings from less-educated, minority, and/or very low-income women, we might have seen a strong preference for the traditional house and neighborhood since they symbolize the social status and security these groups are regularly denied.

Therefore, the fantasy drawings we collected offer only a limited albeit poetic insight into some women's housing choices, for it was the personal and political impact of the workshop on the participants that was most important to us in the 1970s. However, guided drawing exercises can be used for other purposes. Drawings can help break down the barriers between design professionals and low-income client groups, particularly those who speak English as a second language.

For example, in designing Villa Excelsior (see chapter 5), architects from the Women's Development Corporation gave the future residents differently colored and shaped pieces of paper, each symbolizing a certain activity such as sleeping, cooking, or socializing, to create floorplans for their respective apartments. In the process they asked each of the women to define and include a special space of her very own, designated by a heart-shaped piece of paper, which became an important and realizable design criterion. From these collages the architects then developed schematic floorplans for the building. Although this process is difficult and time consuming, it can result in better, more sensitive design solutions and can enhance the self-esteem of the users.

Scholarly research is another purpose for which drawings can be used. In 1984, Jacqueline Leavitt, an urban planner, and Susan Saegert, an environmental psychologist, prepared a housing survey that ran in *Ms.* magazine. Of the 6,000 readers who responded, 808 answered an optional question to draw their ideal house and neighborhood.[23] Leavitt and Saegert are currently writing a book based on the survey results.

Women as Architects of the Future

When women fantasize about dwellings that, like their occupants, can change, grow, think, and respond sensitively to human needs, they are expressing an intuitive understanding of the inextricable connection between the making of places and the making of lives. Living on the periphery of power, marginalized by male-dominated institutions, women have learned to see the world from the outside looking in. The experience of marginality has developed in women the ability to empathize with others, especially the powerless in society. This ability is crucial to the creation of new space that fosters human equality.

Women need to be made aware of their shelter rights and their potential to influence government policy. They need to play more important roles in shaping shelter through participation in all aspects of the housing process—from planning neighborhoods and community developments, to designing, building, selling, and maintaining them, as well as creating public controls such as building and housing codes and housing and redevelopment authorities. They must exercise judgment and make decisions about the nature of the spaces in which they live and work, and endorse those proposals that make life easier for themselves and those groups who have the least.

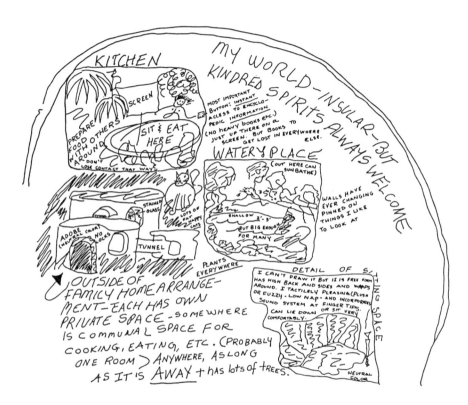

Figure 26. "My World of Kindred Spirits." The full-time homemaker and mother who drew this fantasy placed herself in the kitchen in her "ideal world of kindred spirits," but she included other people and a computer to ensure that the domesticity she finds so pleasurable would not isolate her. This drawing, showing communal spaces and separate but connected private spaces made of adobe and stained glass, is conceptually similar to the college campus and campsite schemes for "individual architecture" described in chapter 6.

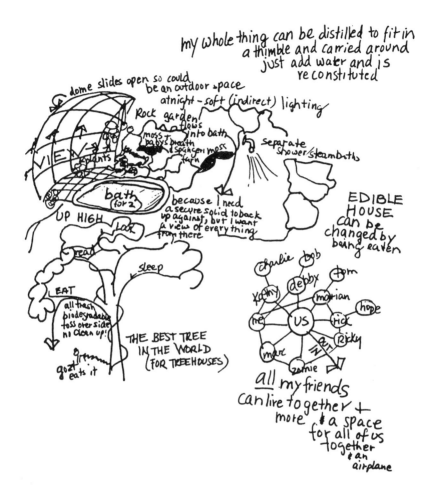

Figure 27. "Edible House." The structure in this image, a fantasy treehouse drawn by a single career woman, can be changed by being eaten, is totally energy efficient and completely portable; it can be "distilled to fit in a thimble and carried around." Each member in the family of friends who lives there ("us") is autonomous yet "related to all the others" (see the diagram in the lower right).

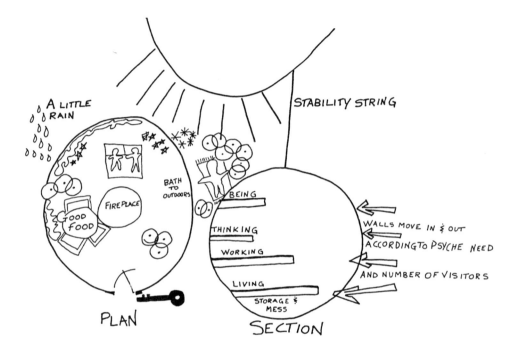

Figure 28. "Existential House." The married woman in her mid-thirties with two children who made this drawing wanted her dream house to change itself in response to her own changing emotional states and practical requirements: "walls move in and out according to psyche needs and the number of visitors." She symbolized her strong need for privacy and control over space by including a large key near the entry to her dwelling (on the left).

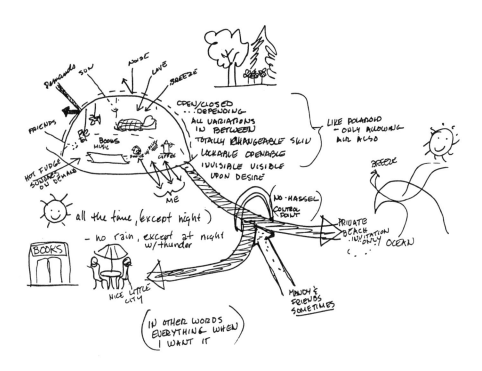

Figure 29. "Marie's Space." Marie, a single parent, designed a permeable dome with a "totally changeable skin" that, like a polaroid lens, responds to the sensory conditions of sunlight and temperature. Demands and noise "bounce off" while love and breezes enter freely. Note the prominent "no hassle control point" in the foreground through which Marie's daughter Mandy and friends must pass in order to enter her home.

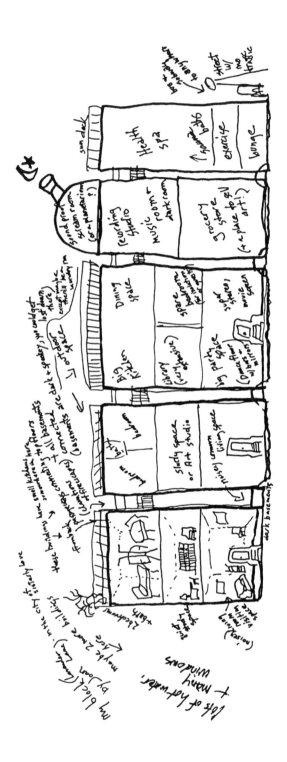

Figure 30. "Congregate Row Housing." The New Yorker who did this drawing connected a city block of private row houses using passageways at the basement and top floor levels. Her renovation is located near good public transportation and includes many shared spaces and support services from an outdoor roof garden, "soundproof scream room and planetarium," music room and recording studio, photographic darkroom, health spa with saunas, a place to sell art, library, and grocery store, to a big communal kitchen-dining room, party space, and guest bedroom. Many of her "fantasies" were included in the architectural programs for real feminist housing projects described and illustrated in chapter 5.

The critical need for affordable shelter is uniting women worldwide in a new, international sisterhood. In 1975, the United Nations opened the Decade for Women, which culminated in a conference in Nairobi in 1985. This historic event illuminated the global prevalence of women's poverty, hunger, illiteracy, and homelessness. Today, there is an increasing realization that the shelter needs of women in developing countries parallel those of low-income women in North America.

From First World slums and public housing projects to Third World squatter settlements, women live in appallingly overcrowded, hazardous, unsanitary dwellings that lack basic facilities—circumstances that worsen daily—exacerbated by global economic recession, military spending, and debt crises that make affordable housing a low priority for many governments. Worldwide poverty among women means that many can afford only limited infrastructural services such as pit latrines, public water hydrants, open drains, and unpaved roads. Lack of adequate sanitation obviously increases health risks.

Women's universally low wages mean that fewer housing units are affordable and that household income is frequently insufficient to meet the eligibility criteria for subsidized housing. The high illiteracy rate among women worldwide limits their access to information about the availability of subsidized housing, typically announced in newspapers and public notices by housing authorities, and the complexity of the application forms and required documentation further prevents many women from being successful applicants. In many countries, women's legal standing denies them the right to own land, which means they cannot protect themselves and their children from domestic instability and violence or provide collateral to gain access to credit or capital. An estimated one-third of the world's households are now headed by women; in parts of Africa and many urban areas, especially in Latin America, the figure is greater than 50 percent, and in the refugee camps in Central America and the public housing projects of North America the figure exceeds 90 percent. Yet the universal favoritism directed toward the male-headed family guarantees that the selection process for recipients of affordable rental and subsidized housing will screen out female-headed households.[24]

Homelessness among women and children, a common and widespread occurrence in many Third World cities, is burgeoning across the United States and Canada. Between 1960 and 1989, major wars have created 25 to 30 million refugees, the majority women and children—especially in Asia, Africa, and Latin America.[25] Women refugees, homeless and often widowed, are systematically subjected to rape in the camps while they await resettlement, an act which is surely a form of political torture. In 1991, the Persian Gulf War caused an estimated 450,000 Kurds to flee from Iraq to the Turkish frontier where they settled in miserable mountain camps. Among the refugees, the children died in particularly large numbers, mostly from malnutrition, exposure, and dehydration.[26]

As women from the First World and Third World countries share their varied housing experiences and strategies, they increase their ability to control their housing and communities, thereby claiming greater control over their own lives, futures, and the welfare of their children. Further, these exchanges can contribute to a growing solidarity among white women and women of color, migrant, native, rural, peasant, displaced, and refugee women, and those whose shelter situation is affected by apartheid in South Africa.

We will not create fully supportive, life-enhancing environments until society values those aspects of human experiences that have been devalued through the oppression of women and other marginalized groups. Concomitantly, successful theories about gender—be they directed toward environmental or any other issues—can emerge only if the experience of all women is really taken into account; and that means recognizing that for many women, race, ethnicity, or class may be at least as significant as gender in their lives.

Toward those ends, much more research is needed that compares the environmental needs of women in developing and more developed countries, explains the differences among ethnic women in urban neighborhoods, and makes visible the isolated worlds of lesbian, disabled, and rural women. We need to know how the divorced mother copes with a suburban environment organized for two-parent nuclear families; how women of different races and classes use workplaces and other public environments such as schools, airports, civic buildings, and parks; and more about why and when women feel safe or theatened in cities and suburbs. To honor women's contributions to society, we must locate and preserve sites of historic importance to women. A feminist award program should be established that acknowledges buildings and community and urban design that support the needs of those who use them as determined by the users themselves.

Architecture exists fundamentally as the expression of an established social order. It is not easily changed until the society that produced it is changed. The scale, complexity, and cost of buildings and human settlements, and the myriad layers of decision making by regulatory authorities, public participation, government, and financial institutions create an overburdened and painfully slow process. Yet the nature of the built environment is such that it can suggest the world transformed as well as the means for its transformation. If we are to design a society in which all people matter, more architects and planners need to become feminists and more feminists need to concern themselves with the design of our physical surroundings.

NOTES

1. James Robertson, "The Future of Work: Some Thoughts about the Roles of Women and Men in the Transition to a SHE Future," *Women's Studies International Quarterly* 4, no. 1 (1981): 83.

2. J. Ray Dettling, "The Amazing Futurephone," *Science Digest,* April 1982, 88.

3. Alvin Toffler, *The Third Wave* (New York: Bantam Books, 1981), 199.

4. "Beginnings of Tomorrow," *Mechanix Illustrated,* January 1981, 107.

5. Carol Barkin, "Electricity Is Her Servant," *Heresies,* "Making Room: Women and Architecture," issue 11, vol. 3, no. 3 (1981): 62–63.

6. Jan Zimmerman, "Technology and the Future of Women: Haven't We Met Somewhere Before?' *Women's Studies International Quarterly* 4, no. 3 (1981): 355–67.

7. Margaret Mead, as quoted in Adele Chatfield-Taylor, "Hitting Home," *Architectural Forum* (March 1973): 60.

8. Betty Friedan, *The Second Stage* (New York: Summit Books, 1981), 281–82.

9. Frances Whyatt, "The Craft of Their Hands," in *Women in Search of Utopia,* ed. Ruby Rohrlich and Elaine Hoffman Baruch (New York: Schocken, 1984), 177–79.

10. Schulamith Firestone, *The Dialectic of Sex: The Case for Feminist Revolution* (New York: Bantam Books, 1970), 231, 234–35.

11. Craig, Kent, and Vicki Hodgetts, "The Birth of Individual Architecture," *Ms.,* Spring 1972, 90–91.

12. Chatfield-Taylor, "Hitting Home," 60.

13. Ibid., 61.

14. Mary Daly, *Beyond God the Father* (Boston: Beacon Press, 1974), 40.

15. Rohrlich and Baruch, *Women in Search of Utopia,* 102–3.

16. Tish Sommers, "Making Changes: Tomorrow Is a Woman's Issue," in *Future, Technology, and Woman, Proceedings of the Conference* (San Diego: San Diego State University, Women's Studies Department, 1981), 71–72.

17. Ibid., 70–72.

18. Margrit Eichler, "Science Fiction as Desirable Feminist Scenarios," *Women's Studies International Quarterly* 4, no. 1 (1981): 51–64.

19. For more information on this project see Noel Phyllis Birkby and Leslie Kanes Weisman, "Patritecture and Feminist Fantasies," *Liberation* 19, nos.

8 and 9 (Spring 1976): 45–52; idem, "Women's Fantasy Environments: Notes on a Project in Process," *Heresies,* "Patterns of Communication and Space among Women," vol. 1, no. 2 (May 1977): 116–17.

20. Noel Phyllis Birkby and Leslie Kanes Weisman, "A Woman-Built Environment: Constructive Fantasies," *Quest, Future Visions* 2, no. 1 (Summer 1975): 17–18.

21. Ibid., 17.

22. These quotes were taken from text included on original drawings in the Birkby-Weisman collection of women's environmental fantasies (1974–76).

23. Jacqueline Leavitt, "The Single Family House: Does It Belong in a Woman's Housing Agenda?," *Shelterforce* (July-September 1989): 8–11.

24. Midgley, *Women's Budget,* 2.

25. Caroline O. N. Moser and Linda Peake, eds., *Women, Human Settlements and Housing* (New York: Tavistock Press, 1987).

26. "Mass Repatriation for Kurds Begins," *New York Times,* 12 May 1991, International section, 9; and Fred R. Conrad, "After the War: A Photographer's Portfolio," *New York Times,* 12 May 1991, International section, 8.

Index